Introduction

CONNECTED series is a four-level course designed for college students who want to use English effectively in their daily lives. This course gives students the opportunity to build up communicative skills through step-by-step learning and practice in each section of every unit. It also provides students with online practice related to the student book and online exercises for TOEIC preparation. Students will learn the four main skills of listening, speaking, reading, and writing in addition to grammar and vocabulary.

There are 12 units in each book, and each unit consists of the following sections:

VOCABULARY

Vocabulary presents general, core, and authentic words and useful expressions in diverse ways. It stimulates students' interest in the theme of the unit. The practices and activities enable students to become familiar with the new words and their proper use.

CONVERSATION

Conversation introduces various real-life conversations among native speakers of English. These sections present key vocabularies used in natural settings allowing students to figure out the meanings using context clues. The conversations should be taken as a starting point for further conversations and help lead the class into further discussions. While some of the language has been simplified the feeling and flavor of the conversation is kept authentic.

GRAMMAR

Grammar introduces essential grammar points to enhance appropriate grammar use and to ensure accuracy. Grammar practices followed by the presentation of grammar points enable students to understand the grammar rules better and advance their grammar skills. This helps students improve accuracy in their spoken and written communication.

READING

Reading passages present high-interest and contemporary topics in many kinds of genres, which are related to the unit theme. A pre-reading question introduces the topic of the reading passage allowing students to think about the topic. Students are also able to enhance their comprehension skills and understand the passages better through the reading comprehension questions followed by the reading passage.

LISTENING

The key to improving one's understanding and mastering a language begins with listening. This section contains diverse real conversations and presents them in a way that helps students understand native speakers. Most of the conversations are focused on the theme of the unit, but there is humor built into it, too. Recognizing and appreciating humor in a second language are just as important as learning the meaning of those dialogues.

SPEAKING

Speaking allows students to learn how to create variations in their speech and keep a conversation exciting. Students cannot express themselves in their own words by just memorizing vocabularies and typical expressions to respond to questions. The activities in this section enable students to practice a variety of language and to apply what they have learned in real-life situations. Language is never static. It is a dynamic dance that must be constantly moving in order to avoid that learned-by-rote feel.

READING SKILL

Reading Skill introduces essential reading skills that students need to develop to succeed in their academic reading. Basic reading skills, such as skimming, scanning, identifying topic sentences and supporting details, using context clues, making inferences, and various other reading skills are presented with practical exercises that help students build up their reading skills.

WRITING

Writing presents a diverse selection of topics to write about. Each writing topic is proceeded by warm-up questions that help students organize their ideas to develop stronger passages. Students are encouraged to review their peers' writings and revise their own writings based on the review from their peers. This will help students write more well-developed passages.

Book 1 Scope & Sequence

Unit	Topic	Vocabulary	Conversation	Grammar
01	I'm from Korea p. 8	Countries and Nationalities	Where Are You from?	*Be* Verb
02	What Do You Do? p. 14	Jobs	Where Do You Work Now?	Simple Present 1: Wh-questions
03	Where Is My Wallet? p. 20	Possessions	I Can't Find My Wallet	Prepositions of Place

Review Units 01~03 p. 26

Unit	Topic	Vocabulary	Conversation	Grammar
04	Whose Car Is This? p. 28	Objects	That's My Car over There	Possessive Adjectives & Possessive Pronouns
05	Is There a Flower Shop around Here? p. 34	Places	How Can I Get to the Flower Shop?	There Is / There Are / Is There? / Are There?
06	I Get up at Seven Every Morning p. 40	Daily Routines	What Time Do You Wake up?	Simple Present 2

Review Units 04~06 p. 46

Unit	Topic	Vocabulary	Conversation	Grammar
07	He's Tall and Muscular p. 48	Physical Appearance	Wow! He Looks Really Handsome	Order of Adjectives
08	What Are You Doing? p. 54	Free Time Activities	What Do You Do in Your Free Time?	Present Progressive
09	Which One Is Prettier? p. 60	Adjectives for Making Comparisons	Is This One Better than That One?	Comparatives / Superlatives

Review Units 07~09 p. 66

Unit	Topic	Vocabulary	Conversation	Grammar
10	What Did You Do This Morning? p. 68	Past Events	What Happened Last Night?	Simple Past
11	I Can Play Tennis p. 74	Hobbies and Abilities	I Love Playing Tennis	*Can* for Ability
12	What Will You Do Next Year? p. 80	Future Plans	Do You Have Plans for Next Year?	Future with *Will*

Review Units 10~12 p. 86

Reading & Reading Skill	Listening & Pronunciation	Speaking	Writing
• My Name is Anna • Scanning for Details	• This Is Kevin • Word Stress	Nice to Meet You!	About Yourself
• Who Wrote Harry Potter? • Skimming	• Tell Me about Your Career • Falling Intonation in Wh-questions	What's Your Occupation?	Your Family Members' Jobs
• My Grandfather's Harmonica • Identifying the Topic and Main Idea	• Lost and Needs to Be Found! • Weak Forms	Where Are They?	Know Your Surroundings
• Materials Make a Difference • Finding Supporting Details	• I'm Looking for My Dog • Plural Ending	Does This Belong to You?	An Item That You Want to Sell or Get Rid of
• Four Major Areas of London • Facts and Opinions	• Oh Man, I'm Lost • Word Stress	Could You Tell Me How to Get There?	Directions to the House Party
• A Wise Blind Woman • Sequencing	• Do You Want to Go on a Date? • Third Person Verb Endings	When Do You Usually Exercise?	My Daily Routine
• Queen Yuna • Scanning for Details	• What Do They Look like? • Linking Sounds: [z] and [ʃ]	Could You Tell Me about Him?	What Makes You Like Someone?
• Kelly's Family on a Weekend • Skimming	• Do You Want to Learn Something New? • Rising and Falling Intonation	Would You Like to Take a Walk?	What Is Your Favorite Free Time Activity?
• Prague, One of the Most Popular Cities in the World • Identifying the Topic and Main Idea	• It's the Most Amazing Thing • Vowel Sounds: [iː], [e], and [ɪ]	I Think the Yellow One Is the Best	Which One Do You Like More?
• The Egyptian Classes and Occupations • Finding Supporting Details	• Where Were They at That Time? • Final -ed of Regular Past Verbs	Did You Do Anything Special?	What a Weekend!
• Soccer Is Popular • Facts and Opinions	• Let's Go See a Game • Voiceless and Voiced Pair: [f] - [v]	Are You Good at Playing Soccer?	What's Your Favorite Sport?
• Robots • Summarizing	• It's My Plan! • Reduced Sound of *going to*	What Are You Planning to Do?	New Year's Resolution

UNIT 01

| Vocabulary
Countries and Nationalities | Conversation
Where Are You from? | Grammar Point
Be Verb | Reading
My Name Is Anna | Listen Up
This Is Kevin | Speaking Build-up
Nice to Meet You! |

I'm from Korea

• Vocabulary • Countries and Nationalities

Online Practice

1. Write the correct name of each country in the blank.

| Korea | Canada | The UK | Germany | Turkey |
| India | Kenya | The US | China | Brazil |

1. _____
2. _____
3. _____
4. _____
5. _____
6. _____
7. _____
8. _____
9. _____
10. _____

2. Match each country with its nationality.

1. Korea •   • German
2. Canada •   • British
3. The UK •   • Korean
4. Germany •   • Turkish
5. Turkey •   • Kenyan
6. India •   • Chinese
7. Kenya •   • Indian
8. The US •   • Canadian
9. China •   • Brazilian
10. Brazil •   • American

Pair Work Practice asking and answering about nationalities.

A: What is your nationality?
B: I'm <u>German</u>.

Conversation • Where Are You from?

1. Look at the picture and describe what is happening.

2. Listen to the conversation and fill in the blanks.

James: Hi, Angela. This is my friend, David. David, this is Angela.
David: Hi. I'm _____ ____ _____ you.
Angela: Nice to meet you. Where are you from?
David: I'm from _____. And you?
Angela: I'm from _____.
David: Do you speak German?
Angela: Only a little, but I understand when someone _____ ____ me in German.
David: That's still very nice.

Pair Work

Practice this dialogue replacing the underlined word.

A: Hello. Where are you from?
B: I'm from Australia.

• Grammar Point • *Be* Verb

Full Forms	Short Forms	Examples
I **am**	I**'m**	I**'m** Sara.
You **are**	You**'re**	You**'re** from Italy.
He **is**	He**'s**	He**'s** happy.
She **is**	She**'s**	She**'s** 18 years old.
It **is**	It**'s**	It**'s** very cold.
We **are**	We**'re**	We**'re** in the living room.
They **are**	They**'re**	They**'re** students.

1. Circle the correct *be* verb.

1. She (am / is / are) 20 years old.
2. Julie and Tony (am / is / are) from Canada.
3. My brother (am / is / are) in the bedroom.
4. You and your friend (am / is / are) Brazilian.
5. It (am / is / are) very nice.

2. Complete the sentences with the correct *be* verbs. Use either full forms or short forms.

1. We _____ teachers.
2. He _____ a Turkish citizen.
3. They _____ American.
4. Lucy _____ from Kenya. She is a cheerful girl.
5. It _____ delicious and smells good.

Pair Work Complete the chart with the information of a certain person. Then take turns telling each other about the person.

Name	Nationality	Age

10 CONNECTED 1

• Reading • My Name Is Anna

1. Look at the title above. Guess what the story is about.

My name is Anna. I am from France. I'm 19 years old. I have long brown hair and blue eyes. I like reading, playing sports, cooking, and watching movies. I also love dogs, but I don't like cats because they make me sneeze.

I came to Korea two years ago. I live with my friend in a small apartment in Bundang. I like living in Korea.

I learn Korean on Tuesdays and Fridays at a college. I also have a part-time job. I teach children English. I work three days a week. I enjoy teaching Korean students.

I can get to the college, which is in Seoul, in 30 minutes by subway or bus. The transportation system in Korea is fast and easy.

[**Reading Skill:** Scanning for Details] Go to Page 88.

2. Read the passage. Write *T* for true or *F* for false for each statement.

1. Anna lives with her friend in France. _____
2. She learns Korean twice a week at a college. _____
3. The transportation system in Korea is difficult and slow. _____

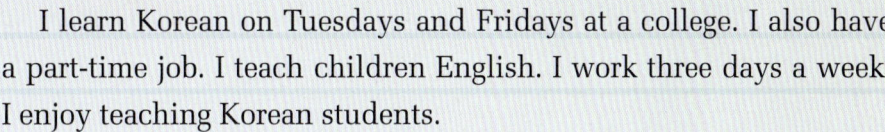

Group Work

Discuss this question in a group.

- What do you say when you introduce yourself to others?

• Listen Up • This Is Kevin

1. Getting Ready Listen and study the way people say phone numbers and email addresses.

> **251-5478:** two-five-one, five-four-seven-eight
> **018-2134-5202:** oh-one-eight, two-one-three-four, five-two-oh-two
> zero-one-eight, two-one-three-four, five-two-zero-two
> **dream71@pagoda.com:** dream-seven-one-*at*-pagoda-*dot*-com
> **sung-su@connected.com:** sung-*hyphen*-su-*at*-connected-*dot*-com / sung-*dash*-su-*at*-connected-*dot*-com

2. Easy Listening Listen to the dialogue and complete the chart.

Name	Phone Number
Alice	
John	

3. Hard Rock Listen to the radio show and answer the questions.

1. Who is the first person WTMI Radio show presents?
   a. Barack Obama
   b. Barack Obama's mother

2. What did Obama do before he became the President of the United States?
   a. He was a lawyer and professor.
   b. He was a senator and doctor.

4. Pronunciation Word Stress
Listen and practice. Notice where the stress falls on in each word.

Kor**é**a	C**á**nada	**É**ngland
Braz**í**l	T**ú**rkey	**Í**ndia

12 CONNECTED 1

Speaking Build-up • Nice to Meet You!

1. Study the expressions for saying hello.

A: Hello, what's going on?
B: Not much. How are you?
A: Great! Is she your friend?
B: Yes, this is my friend, Jenny.
C: Hi, I'm Jenny. Glad to meet you!
A: I'm Robert. It's nice to meet you!

A:
- Hi! / Greetings!
- What's going on?
- What's up?

C:
- (It's) Nice to meet you!
- (It's) A pleasure to meet you!

2. Complete the chart.

	Japan	Germany	Spain	Canada
Nationality				
Language				
Money				

Pair Work

Practice this dialogue using the chart above.

A: Nice to meet you! Are you from Brazil?
B: Yes, I'm from Brazil.
A: What language do you speak?
B: I speak Portuguese.
A: What kind of money do you use in Brazil?
B: We use *Real* [reɪá:l].

Culture Awareness — Mixed Origins

It has become politically correct to identify your origin when talking about being from a certain country or area of the world. It is common to hear that someone is African-American. If a person is born from African parents in the United States, he or she would be African-American.

Tips Some subjects that are considered taboo: age, weight, religion, abortion, equality among sexes, sexual preference, sex, money, or family history

[Writing: About Yourself] Go to Page 89.

UNIT 02 What Do You Do?

Vocabulary	Conversation	Grammar Point	Reading	Listen Up	Speaking Build-up
Jobs	Where Do You Work Now?	Simple Present 1: Wh-questions	Who Wrote Harry Potter?	Tell Me about Your Career	What's Your Occupation?

• Vocabulary •   Jobs

 Online Practice

1. Choose the correct word for each picture and write the letter.

a. doctor	b. instructor	c. police officer	d. actor	e. designer
f. taxi driver	g. photographer	h. computer programmer	i. singer	j. chef

2. Match each word with its definition.

1. actor • • a person who cooks food for others
2. designer • • a person who acts in a play or a movie
3. chef • • a person who has the job of designing things

 Pair Work

Practice asking and answering about jobs.

> **A:** What do you do?
> **B:** I'm a designer.

• **Conversation** • **Where Do You Work Now?**

1. Look at the picture and describe what is happening.

2. Listen to the conversation and fill in the blanks.

Bob: Hello, Mary. Long time no see.

Mary: Oh, hi, Bob! It is _____ _____ _____ _____. How are you?

Bob: Just fine. I remember you work at Florence Hospital as a _____.
Do you still work there?

Mary: No, I moved to Charity Hospital. It's downtown. Where do you work now?

Bob: Oh, I have my own company as a _____ _____.

Mary: Really? Where is your office?

Bob: I usually work _____ _____, but I can work anywhere.

👥 Pair Work

Practice this dialogue replacing the underlined words.

> **A:** Long time no see! Are you still a graduate student?
> **B:** No, I'm not. I work at a bank. How about you?
> **A:** I work at a restaurant. I'm a chef.

Unit 02 What Do You Do?

• Grammar Point • Simple Present 1: Wh-questions

Wh-questions with *do*: **Wh-word** + *do/does* + Subject + *Verb*...?
Wh-questions with *be*: **Wh-word** + *be* + Subject...?

Wh-questions	Answers
What *is* that?	It *is* a computer.
Who *do* you *live* with?	I *live* with my friend.
When *is* the game?	It *is* 5 p.m. this afternoon.
Where *does* he *live*?	He *lives* in Seoul.
Why *are* you happy?	I*'m* happy because I won the prize.
How *are* you?	I*'m* good.

1. Complete the sentences with the correct wh-words: *what, who, when, where, why*, or *how*.

1. _____ do you live?
2. _____ do you work with?
3. _____ is the weather?
4. _____ is your birthday?
5. _____ is your name?
6. _____ are you crying?

2. Make wh-questions in simple present.

1. (Where / you / go to school?) _____
2. (Where / John / work?) _____
3. (How long / it / take to get to Paris?) _____
4. (How often / she / go to the movies?) _____
5. (How many children / you / have?) _____

 **Pair Work**

Practice these dialogues replacing the underlined words.

A: Where do you <u>work</u>?
B: I <u>work at a hospital</u>.

A: When does he <u>go to school</u>?
B: He <u>goes to school at 8</u>.

Reading • Who Wrote Harry Potter?

1. Look at the title above and the picture below. What do you think the woman's job is?

J. K. Rowling is the famous writer of the Harry Potter fantasy series. She was born in Yate, England in 1965. She came up with the idea for the Harry Potter stories while she was on a train that was delayed for several hours.

It was not an easy job to write the stories. She was poor and had a daughter to take care of. She wrote by hand because she didn't have enough money to buy a typewriter or a computer.

In 1997, her first book, *Harry Potter and the Sorcerer's Stone* was published in the UK. In the book, Harry Potter is a young wizard in training at the Hogwarts School. Rowling wrote six more books in the series. The seventh book was printed in about 200 countries and 60 languages. The books have been made into a movie series that is famous all over the world.

[Reading Skill: Skimming] Go to Page 90.

2. Read the passage. Write *T* for true or *F* for false for each statement.

1. J. K. Rowling worked on the idea for the Harry Potter stories for years. _____
2. Rowling couldn't afford to buy a typewriter or a computer. _____
3. The seventh Harry Potter book was sold in about 300 countries. _____

Group Work

Discuss this question in a group.

- What is the ideal occupation you want to have in the future?

Listen Up • Tell Me about Your Career

1. Getting Ready Match each word with its definition.

1. busboy • • a person who roasts and brews coffee
2. barista • • a person who cleans up the tables
3. babysitter • • a person who takes care of babies and young children
4. cashier • • a person who helps find books at the library
5. librarian • • a person who checks out things at a market

2. Easy Listening Listen to the dialogue and answer the questions.

1. What is NOT one of the part-time jobs he does?
   a. a busboy   b. a babysitter
   c. a barista   d. a librarian

2. When does he work in the cafeteria?
   a. on Mondays, Wednesdays, and Fridays
   b. on Tuesdays and Thursdays

3. Hard Rock Listen to the interview and answer the questions.

1. What job did Darrell have when he was 18 years old?
   a. a soldier   b. a purchasing manager

2. Where did he work as a purchasing manager?
   a. at military   b. at a hospital

3. Darrell worked different _____ _____ as a teenager, but now he works _____ _____.

*odd jobs: small tasks that are usually paid per job

4. Pronunciation Falling Intonation in Wh-questions
Listen and practice. Notice the voice tone goes down at the end of the questions.

| What do you do? | Who are they? | How is the weather? |
| Where do you live? | Why are you happy? | When is the party? |

• Speaking Build-up • What's Your Occupation?

1. Study the expressions to talk about jobs.

A: <u>What kind of work do you do</u>?
B: I'm an office woman.
A: Do you like your job?
B: Not really. I want to do something interesting.
A: <u>What would be your dream job</u>?
B: I want to be a hair designer.

A
- What's your occupation / job?
- What do you do for a living?
- What company do you work for?

A
- What job would you most like to do?
- What is the job you most want?

2. Complete the chart by filling in your own answers.

Questions about a dream job	e.g.) Mark	You
What would be your dream job?	product manager	
Where do you want to work?	Apple Inc.	
What time do you want to start and finish work?	anytime I want	
How many days a week do you want to work?	5 days	
How many hours a day do you want to work?	8 hours	

 Pair Work

Practice asking and answering questions about your dream jobs using the chart above.

A: What would be your dream job? <u>Where do you want to work?</u>
B: I want to be a <u>product manager</u>. I want to work at <u>Apple Inc</u>.

Culture Awareness — Job Esteem

Different jobs hold different levels of respect around the world. From country to country, the level of importance can change dramatically. In Asia, teachers are held as a very important and honored position. On the other hand, in America, doctors and lawyers are usually the more prestigious jobs.

[Writing: Your Family Members' Jobs] Go to Page 91.

UNIT 03

Vocabulary	Conversation	Grammar Point	Reading	Listen Up	Speaking Build-up
Possessions	I Can't Find My Wallet	Prepositions of Place	My Grandfather's Harmonica	Lost and Needs to Be Found!	Where Are They?

Where Is My Wallet?

• Vocabulary • Possessions

Online Practice

1. Choose the correct word for each picture and write the letter.

a. planner	b. mechanical pencil	c. DSLR	d. wallet	e. bike
f. glasses	g. laptop computer	h. backpack	i. cell phone	j. CDs

2. Fill in the blanks with the correct words from the box above.

1. I forgot to bring my _____. I have no money.
2. Would you use a pencil or a _____ to mark the correct answers?
3. These photos were taken by a _____. They are all great.

**Pair Work**

Practice asking and answering about possessions.

A: What do you have in your bag?
B: In my bag, I have <u>a cell phone and a wallet</u>.

20 CONNECTED 1

• Conversation • I Can't Find My Wallet

UNIT | 03

1. Look at the picture and describe what is happening.

2. Listen to the conversation and fill in the blanks.

Peter: What's wrong, Wendy?

Wendy: I can't find my _____.

Peter: Really? When did you have it last?

Wendy: That's the problem. I don't remember.

Peter: Is it _____ _____ _____?

Wendy: No, that's the _____ place I looked. And I checked here and there, but I can't find it.

Peter: Well, what did you do yesterday?

Wendy: I was shopping online, and I needed my _____ _____ ...

Peter: Is that it? Next to the _____?

Wendy: That's it! Thank you.

👥 Pair Work

Practice this dialogue replacing the underlined words.

A: Where did you put your <u>bag</u>? **B:** I put it <u>under the chair</u>.

Unit 03 Where Is My Wallet?   21

Grammar Point • Prepositions of Place

Prepositions	Examples
in	I watch TV **in** the living room.
at	I met her **at** the entrance.
on	The cat is **on** the chair.
by / next to / beside	The bank is **by/next to/beside** the school.
between	The pen is **between** the book and the camera.
behind	I put my bike **behind** the door.
in front of	She started talking to the man **in front of** her.
under	The pen is **under** the chair.

1. Fill in the blanks with the correct prepositions from the box.

| under | in | on | in front of | by |

1. Sign your name _____ the line.
2. A cat is sleeping _____ the bridge.
3. I want to sit _____ you at the movie theater.
4. My grandmother is reading _____ the living room.
5. Your glasses are right _____ you, not behind you.

2. Complete the sentences with the correct prepositions.

1. The bakery is _____ the first floor.
2. We had a great time _____ the concert.
3. Many students are standing _____ line.
4. I study hard _____ school.
5. He is not _____ the office. He is out for lunch.

Pair Work

Practice this dialogue replacing the underlined words.

A: Where is my <u>cell phone</u>?
B: It's <u>on the table</u>.

Reading • My Grandfather's Harmonica

1. Look at the picture. What do you think the passage is about?

Some of my best memories from my childhood are the ones of spending the weekends on my grandparents' farm. My cousins and I would spend the days playing in the barn. My favorite memory is my grandfather's harmonica playing.

We would sit around the fire and he'd sit in his old chair. He wore his old T-shirt smelling of hay and gasoline and played "the good old hymns".

My grandfather taught us a lot about the harmonica. I still remember Ben Franklin was the first American to invent an important musical instrument – the glass harmonica.

As my grandfather gets older, it's harder for him to play the harmonica. But he still carries it in his pocket every day. He says it is the most important thing in his life. That's important for us, too.

[Reading Skill: Identifying the Topic and Main Idea] Go to Page 92.

2. Read the passage and answer the following questions.

1. What did the writer NOT do at his grandparents' farm?
   - a. playing in the barn
   - b. feeding the chickens
   - c. listening to the harmonica
   - d. sitting around the fire

2. What was the writer's favorite memory from childhood?
   - a. his grandfather's harmonica playing
   - b. making a glass harmonica
   - c. his grandfather's old chair
   - d. his grandfather's old T-shirt

3. Who was the first American that invented the glass harmonica?
   - a. Frank Sinatra
   - b. Ben Franklin
   - c. Fred Harmonica
   - d. the writer's grandfather

 **Group Work**

Discuss this question in a group.

- What was the most precious possession you had when you were a child?

• **Listen Up** • **Lost and Needs to Be Found!**

1. Getting Ready Listen and write the letter on the correct picture.

1.  2.  3.  4.  5.

2. Easy Listening Listen to the dialogue and answer the questions.

1. What is the woman looking for?
   a. her glasses
   b. her goggles

2. Where were the glasses located?
   a. on top of her computer
   b. on top of her head

3. Hard Rock Listen to the dialogue and answer the questions.

1. What will they shop for?
   a. Christmas presents
   b. wedding presents

2. Who are they going to buy the watch for?
   a. Johnny
   b. Mike

3. Where does the woman suggest to go shopping?
   a. at Harrods'
   b. at the mall

4. Pronunciation Weak Forms
Listen and practice. Notice the sounds of unstressed words.

> I went **to the** shop **to** buy a wallet.

• Speaking Build-up • Where Are They?

1. Study the expressions to talk about where things are.

A: Did you see my watch?
B: No. Have you looked in your room?
A: Yes, I did. But it wasn't there. I wonder where it is.
B: Do you remember when you last saw it?
A: Not at all. Where can I look for it?
B: Why don't you check your pockets?

A
- Where did I leave it?
- Where can I look for it?
- Where did I put it?

B
- Check your pockets.
- Have you checked your bag?

2. Look at the picture. Choose six items and write the items in the chart.

Items	

Pair Work

Practice this dialogue using the picture and the chart above.

A: Where is the computer located?
B: It's on the desk between two speakers.

Culture Awareness — Lost and Found

When you lose one of your personal items, do not frustrate yet but go to a nearest lost and found. You may retrieve it from the office, only if the person who found the item is kind enough to return it back to its clumsy owner. Just in case you may lose one, try to put a personal identifier onto your items. That way, you can be less worried that you won't find any of your lost items forever.

[Writing: Know Your Surroundings] Go to Page 93.

Review Units 01~03

• Conversation • Welcome to the U.S.

Listen to the conversation and fill in the blanks.

Officer: Welcome to the United States, may I see your passport?
Peter: Sure, here you are.
Officer: It says you are _____ _____. Are you here on business or pleasure?
Peter: Business, unfortunately.
Officer: What kind of business are you in?
Peter: I am in _____ _____ _____ _____. I work for _____ _____ _____ _____.
Officer: Okay. May I see your return ticket, please?
Peter: Sure… Wait… I just had it. It's not in my pocket. _____ _____ _____ _____ _____?
Officer: Sir?
Peter: Yes?
Officer: Sir, it's in _____ _____ _____ with your jacket.
Peter: Oh, thank you so much. Here you are.
Officer: Welcome to the United States.

Pair Work

Role-play a conversation between a customs agent and a visiting tourist using the chart below.

Name	Jamie Bond	Natasha Romanov
Country	The U.S.	Russia
Occupation	salesperson	teacher
Purpose of Visit	visiting a friend	sightseeing

26 CONNECTED 1

Reading • David Beckham, a Superstar!

Read the passage and choose the best answer to each question.

David Beckham is one of the most famous soccer players in the world today. He was born in 1975, in London, England. He is a great midfielder and also has amazing shooting skills. He is able to bend a shot around players who are standing to defend against the free kick.

When he was 11, he won a soccer contest. Manchester United, one of England's best teams, soon took an interest in his ability. Beckham played for Manchester United's youth team. He led the team to a national championship in 1992. Finally, Beckham joined the professional Manchester United team in 1995. He made a great contribution to the team to win six Premier League championships. In 2003, Beckham left Manchester United and moved to Spain and joined Real Madrid.

As a member of England national football team, he played in the World Cup tournament three times: in 1998, 2002, and 2006. But the results weren't good enough for him and the team. Argentina beat England in the second round in 1998. England got into the quarter finals in 2002 and 2006, but they lost to Brazil and Portugal. However, he is the English player that scored the most goals in three World Cups. He was the captain of the England national football team for seven years from 2000.

1. **What is the passage mainly about?**
   a. David Beckham's soccer career at Manchester United
   b. David Beckham's life and his soccer career
   c. David Beckham's career as a captain of the England national football team
   d. David Beckham's family and work history

2. **When did David Beckham join Real Madrid?**
   a. in 1992   b. in 1995   c. in 2003   d. in 2006

3. **What is the main topic of the second paragraph?**
   a. David Beckham's accomplishments in soccer teams
   b. David Beckham's success and failure in the World Cup
   c. David Beckham's life as a celebrity
   d. David Beckham's youth

4. **To which country did England lose their game in 1998?**
   a. Germany   b. Brazil   c. Argentina   d. Italy

| UNIT 04 | Vocabulary
Objects | Conversation
That's My Car over There | Grammar Point
Possessive Adjectives & Possessive Pronouns | Reading
Materials Make a Difference | Listen Up
I'm Looking for My Dog | Speaking Build-up
Does This Belong to You? |

Whose Car Is This?

• Vocabulary • Objects

 Online Practice

1. Choose the correct word for each object and write the letter.

a. car

b. couch

c. jacket

d. basketball

e. DVD

f. sneakers

g. coffee machine

h. guitar

i. hat

j. refrigerator

2. Choose the word that is NOT related to each object.

1. **couch**   a. soft   b. wooden   c. relaxing   d. comfortable
2. **basketball**   a. round   b. flying   c. bouncing   d. leather
3. **refrigerator** a. rectangular b. cooling   c. wheels   d. freezing

 Pair Work

Practice this dialogue replacing the underlined words.

A: Whose <u>jacket</u> is this?

B: It is <u>my jacket</u>.

• **Conversation** • **That's My Car over There**

1. Look at the picture and describe what is happening.

2. Listen to the conversation and fill in the blanks.

Wilma: Is this Fred's car?
Betty: Well, he said it was a big black car.
Wilma: Look inside! What a mess!
Betty: There're a _____ and some old _____ in the front seat.
Wilma: The back seat is covered with _____ _____.
Betty: I'm not sure if getting a ride is a good idea.
Fred: Hello, are you ready to go?
Wilma: Uh, sure, shall we get in…?
Fred: Yep… But that's my car over there.
Betty: Oh, thank heavens… Do you know whose _____ this is?
Fred: I think it belongs to Barney.

Pair Work

Practice this dialogue replacing the underlined words.

A: Which is <u>your car</u>?
B: <u>My car</u> is <u>the big blue one</u>.

Grammar Point • Possessive Adjectives & Possessive Pronouns

Possessive Adjectives	Possessive Pronouns	Examples
my	mine	If the book belongs to me, it is **my** book. It is **mine**.
your	yours	If the pants belong to you, they are **your** pants. They are **yours**.
her	hers	If the earrings belong to her, they are **her** earrings. They are **hers**.
his	his	If the watch belongs to him, it is **his** watch. It is **his**.
its	–	If the bone belongs to the dog, it is **its** bone.
our	ours	If the car belongs to us, it is **our** car. It is **ours**.
their	theirs	If the food belongs to them, it is **their** food. It is **theirs**.

1. Circle the correct words.

1. Jenny's dad cleans the car. (Its / It's) windows are clear.
2. You must clean (your / yours) room before you go to the party.
3. Mr. and Mrs. Rochester bought a plant for (their / theirs) house.
4. The bike over there is (him / his), but this one here is (my / mine).
5. Angela likes to wear (her / hers) hair long while Peggy prefers to wear (her / hers) short.

2. Complete the sentences with the correct possessives.

1. My son did _____ homework without my help. He did it by himself.
2. Pick any of these desserts. The choice is _____ .
3. He loves the book. _____ pictures and stories are great.
4. All my brothers love video games. Playing them is _____ favorite thing to do.
5. **A:** Whose candy is it? **B:** It's _____ . I bought it yesterday.

 **Pair Work**

Practice asking and answering about to whom things belong.

> **A:** Is this cell phone yours?
> **B:** No, it's not mine. I think it is Johnny's.

Reading • Materials Make a Difference

1. Look at the graph. What do you think it shows?

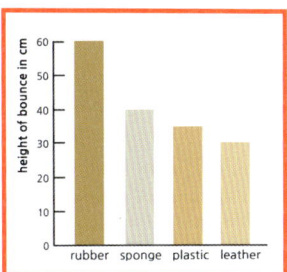

All objects are made of things. These things are called "materials". There are many kinds of materials including leather, stone, wood, plastic, glass, and rubber. They can be used in different ways.

However, proper materials have to be used for items. For example, you can't play a stone guitar because it's too heavy. DVDs cannot be made of rubber. A wooden pillow is not very comfortable. It is important to use the right materials to make things better and more useful.

Let's take an example of a ball. What materials can be used to make a ball? Look at the graph. Can you see the different materials used? There are rubber, sponge, plastic, and leather. Balls made of each material bounce different heights. We can see which one is the bounciest.

What does "bounciest" mean then? Does it mean the ball bounces the highest? Or does it mean the ball bounces for the longest time? The bar graph shows the results. The rubber ball dropped down from a place one meter high bounces 60 centimeters high. The plastic ball bounces over 30 centimeters while the leather ball bounces 30 centimeters. Therefore, if you want to make the bounciest ball, make sure to use rubber. Always remember that different materials make all the difference.

[**Reading Skill:** Finding Supporting Details] Go to Page 94.

2. Read the passage and answer the following questions.

1. What is the passage mainly about?
   - a. different kinds of materials
   - b. how balls are made
   - c. the height of bouncing
   - d. how materials affect bounciness

2. Which is NOT true about the passage?
   - a. We can't play a stone guitar because it's too heavy.
   - b. The sponge ball can bounce almost 50 centimeters high.
   - c. DVDs can't be made of rubber.
   - d. The rubber ball bounces 60 centimeters high.

3. What does "bounciest" mean?
   - a. bouncing the highest
   - b. bouncing for the longest time
   - c. bouncing the lowest
   - d. bouncing for the shortest time

Group Work

Discuss this question in a group.

- If you can change some materials of an object or an item, what would you like to change and why?

Listen Up • I'm Looking for My Dog

1. Getting Ready Learn the meaning of each word.

> **block:** to prevent anything from moving
> **look for:** to try to find someone or something
> **missing:** not in its usual place

2. Easy Listening Listen to the dialogue and answer the questions.

1. What did the woman think was the problem at first?
   a. Her car windows were open.
   b. Her car was blocking another car.

2. What did the man do to the car?
   a. covered the windows with plastic
   b. rolled up the car windows

3. Hard Rock Listen to the radio show and answer the questions.

1. Where was the dog last seen?
   a. in the main square
   b. on the main street

2. What is NOT true about the dog?
   a. missing left leg
   b. last seen Friday afternoon

3. What is the name of the dog?
   a. Lefty
   b. Lucky

4. Pronunciation Plural Ending
Listen and practice. Notice the [iz] sound at the end of the plural nouns.

glass-glass**es**	house-hous**es**	watch-watch**es**
box-box**es**	wish-wish**es**	piece-piec**es**

Speaking Build-up • Does This Belong to You?

1. Study the expressions to talk about to whom things belong.

A: Do you know whose book this is?
B: It's not mine. Maybe it's his.
A: Is this yours?
C: Yes, I have been looking everywhere for it.
   Where did you find it?
A: I found it on my desk, just a while ago.
B: Thank you so much.
A: No problem.

A
- Does this belong to you?
- I think this might be yours.

C
- Where was it?
- Thank heavens, you found it.

2. Find to whom each object belongs. Write the name of the person in the blank.

Martha Hubbard – housewife
Jamie Understood – student
Carl Fixit – car mechanic
Daisy Buchanan – millionaire
Justin Case – plumber
Peter Gunn – photographer

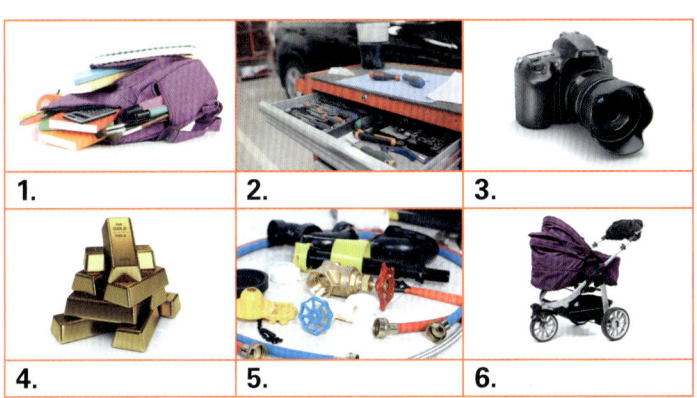

1.   2.   3.
4.   5.   6.

👥 Pair Work

Practice this dialogue using the chart above.

A: Do you know whose bag this is?
B: It is Jamie Understood's.

Culture Awareness   **Secondhand Sale**

Many westerners have fun searching for secondhand items at rummage sales or in classified ads in the newspaper. Often you can get a good deal, but you must be careful not to buy a lemon. Buying a lemon means that you have paid more money than it is actually worth.

*secondhand: previously owned or used

[Writing: An Item That You Want to Sell or Get Rid of] Go to Page 95.

UNIT 05

Vocabulary	Conversation	Grammar Point	Reading	Listen Up	Speaking Build-up
Places	How Can I Get to the Flower Shop?	There Is / There Are Is There? / Are There?	Four Major Areas of London	Oh Man, I'm Lost	Could You Tell Me How to Get There?

Is There a Flower Shop around Here?

• Vocabulary • Places

1. Choose and write the correct word for each place.

> park   jewelry store   convenience store   dentist   movie theater   mall

1. _____
2. _____
3. _____
4. _____
5. _____
6. _____

2. Fill in the blanks with the correct words from the box above.

1. Let's play catch, and walk around at the _____ on Sunday!
2. I'm at a _____ to buy snacks, drinks, and ice cream.
3. To have your teeth examined, you should go to the _____.

Pair Work

Practice this dialogue replacing the underlined words.

> A: Is there <u>a dentist</u> around here?
> B: Yes, there is.

34   CONNECTED 1

• Conversation • **How Can I Get to the Flower Shop?**

1. Look at the picture and describe what is happening.

2. Listen to the conversation and fill in the blanks.

Diana: Excuse me. Is there a _____ _____ around here?
Kevin: Yes, there's one around the corner.
Diana: I'm new to the area. Could you be a little more specific?
Kevin: Sure, walk straight and turn left at the corner. You'll see a big _____ _____. The flower shop is _____ the convenience store and the bank.
Diana: Oh, thanks. One more question… Is there a _____ _____ nearby?
Kevin: I'm not sure, but ask Cathy in the flower shop. She can help.
Diana: Thanks so much.

Pair Work

Ask and answer about the location of a place using the words given.

community center - in front of the hospital	parking area - across from the bakery
bookstore - between the drugstore and the bank	cafeteria - behind the shopping mall

A: Where is the playground?   **B:** It's next to the cafeteria.

Unit 05 Is There a Flower Shop around Here?   35

• Grammar Point • There Is / There Are / Is There? / Are There?

Statements		Questions	
Affirmative	**Negative**	**Yes-No Questions**	**Wh-questions**
There is one desk in the room.	**There is not (isn't)** a dog in the room.	**Is there** a flower shop in the mall? Yes, **there is**. No, **there isn't**.	How many books **are there** in the library?
There are four students in the classroom.	**There are not (aren't)** any books on the desk.	**Are there** many people in the bookstore? Yes, **there are**. No, **there aren't**.	How many people **are there** in your group?

1. Circle the correct words.

1. There (is / are) a school next to the bookstore.
2. There (is / are) many coffee shops around here.
3. (Is / Are) there any hospitals near here?
4. There (isn't / aren't) any train station in this town.
5. There (isn't / aren't) any movies that I want to see at the theater.

2. Unscramble the words and complete the sentences.

1. a teacher / There / is / in / town / the / .
   _____

2. a school / near / here / Is / there / ?
   _____

3. restaurants / in / this / city /There / aren't / many / .
   _____

 Pair Work

Practice this dialogue replacing the underlined words.

A: How many <u>dentists</u> are there in this town?
B: There <u>is</u> <u>one dentist</u>.

Reading • Four Major Areas of London

1. Have you ever been to London? What do you know about London?

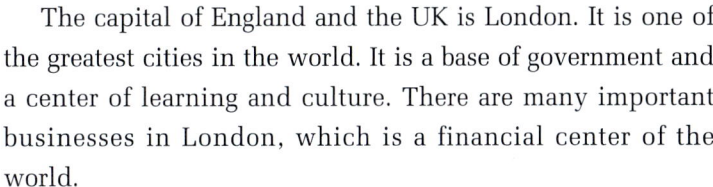

The capital of England and the UK is London. It is one of the greatest cities in the world. It is a base of government and a center of learning and culture. There are many important businesses in London, which is a financial center of the world.

London has four major areas. The oldest section of London is called The City. It covers the area from the Tower of London to Fleet Street. There are many financial and business buildings in The City. Beginning with Fleet Street and ending with Hyde Park, everything in between is called The West End. There are the Houses of Parliament, Whitehall, Buckingham Palace, the University of London, as well as many museums and galleries in this area. The East End is east of the Tower. There is the port of London and there are also many large industrial and housing areas. The South Bank is south of the Thames River, between Lambeth and Tower Bridge. Several important buildings and skyscrapers, housing areas, government offices, and private companies are there. London is also famous for its parks. There is Kensington Gardens, Hyde Park, Green Park, St. James Park, and Regent's Park.

[Reading Skill: Facts and Opinions] Go to Page 96.

2. Read the passage and answer the following questions.

1. **What is the main idea of the passage?**
   a. London has four major areas.
   b. There are many gardens in London.
   c. London is the capital of England.
   d. London is one of the greatest cities.

2. **Which is NOT one of the four major areas of London?**
   a. The West End
   b. Hyde Park
   c. The South Bank
   d. The City

3. **What is NOT true about The City?**
   a. There are government offices.
   b. It stretches from Fleet Street to the Tower of London.
   c. It is the oldest part of London.
   d. There are many financial and business buildings.

Group Work

Discuss these questions in a group.

- Where is your favorite place in the world and why is it your favorite?
- Where is the most memorable place you've visited?

• Listen Up • **Oh Man, I'm Lost**

1. Getting Ready Number the sentences to give the correct directions to the destination.

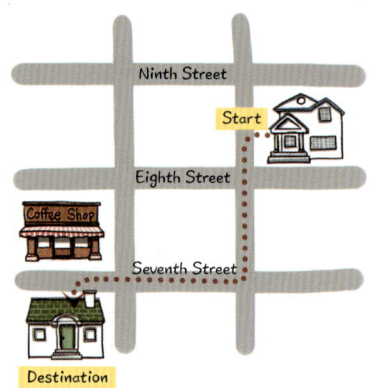

How can I get to my destination?

( ) It's on your left, across from the coffee shop.

( ) When you get to the Seventh Street, turn right.

( ) Walk one block down to Seventh Street.

( ) Go straight one block.

2. Easy Listening Listen to the dialogue and answer the questions.

1. What is the person looking for?
   a. a taxi cab stand
   b. a movie theater

2. Where is the taxi cab stand?
   a. in front of the bank
   b. next to the bank

3. Where is the movie theater?
   a. behind the person
   b. next to the post office

3. Hard Rock Listen to the advertisement and answer the questions.

1. What is the maximum discount available to all customers?
   a. 10%
   b. 25%

2. What do the first 100 customers have a chance to win on Friday?
   a. discounted electronics
   b. 50% off coupons

4. Pronunciation Word Stress

Listen and practice. Notice where the stress falls on in each word.

bookstore	a**cross**	pa**ja**mas
beautiful	re**view**	to**ma**to
jacket	under**stand**	fan**tas**tic

• Speaking Build-up • Could You Tell Me How to Get There?

1. Study the expressions for asking directions.

   A: Would you please tell me where a bank is?
   B: Sorry, I don't know where it is.
   A: Okay… Excuse me. I'm lost. Will you help me?
   C: Sure, where are you going?
   A: I'm looking for a bank.
   C: Oh, it's right over there, across the street.
   A: Thank you.

   - Would you please tell me where…?
   - Where is / are…?
   - I'm looking for…
   - Do you know where…?
   - Can you help me (to) find…?

2. Draw a map of your neighborhood including your house and six other places.

   My Neighborhood

 Pair Work

Practice this dialogue using the map you've made above.

A: Is there a drugstore in your neighborhood?
B: Yes, there is.
A: How can I get there from your house?
B: Go straight for one block to east and turn left. It's on your right.

Culture Awareness — Tourist

Don't be afraid to ask for help. A map is the surest way to be marked as a tourist. It will usually help you get assistance in looking for a place. If you want to blend in, you should use your smartphone and download a map application. Most of the time, the directions are accurate, but you should still ask people if you are lost.

[Writing: Directions to the House Party] Go to Page 97.

UNIT 06

Vocabulary	Conversation	Grammar Point	Reading	Listen Up	Speaking Build-up
Daily Routines	What Time Do You Wake up?	Simple Present 2	A Wise Blind Woman	Do You Want to Go on a Date?	When Do You Usually Exercise?

I Get up at Seven Every Morning

• Vocabulary • Daily Routines

Online Practice

1. Choose the correct word for each picture and write the letter.

> **a.** get up **b.** talk over coffee **c.** have lunch **d.** read a book **e.** send a text message
> **f.** talk on the phone **g.** check email **h.** take a shower **i.** go jogging **j.** watch TV

2. Unscramble the words and complete the sentences.

1. every / morning / get / I / up / seven / at / .

   _____

2. have / at / lunch / o'clock / one / They / .

   _____

3. evening / TV / I / watch / the / in / .

   _____

 **Pair Work**

Practice this dialogue replacing the underlined words.

> **A:** What do you do after <u>your English class</u>?
> **B:** I <u>talk over coffee with my classmates</u>.

• Conversation • What Time Do You Wake up?

1. Look at the picture and describe what is happening.

2. Listen to the conversation and fill in the blanks.

Jared: Why are you late today?
Gemma: Honestly, I _____ _____ late.
Jared: What time do you usually _____ _____ in the morning?
Gemma: I get up at seven every morning.
Jared: What time do you leave for work?
Gemma: I usually _____ _____ 8:15.
Jared: Do you take the bus or the subway to get here?
Gemma: I _____ _____ _____.
Jared: Try taking the subway. It is usually faster than the bus.
Gemma: Okay, I'll try that tomorrow.

Pair Work

Ask and answer about your daily routines.

> **A:** What time do you have lunch?
> **B:** I usually have lunch around 1 o'clock.

Grammar Point • Simple Present 2

Statements		Questions	
Affirmative	**Negative**	**Yes-No questions**	**Wh-questions**
I/You/We/They **play** tennis every Tuesday.	I/You/We/They **don't play** tennis every Tuesday.	**Do** you/they **play** tennis every Tuesday?	**Where do** you/they **play** tennis every Tuesday?
He/She **plays** tennis every Tuesday.	He/She **doesn't play** tennis every Tuesday.	**Does** he/she **play** tennis every Tuesday?	**Where Does** he/she **play** tennis every Tuesday?
The sun (It) **rises** in the east.	The sun (It) **doesn't rise** in the west.	**Does** the sun (it) **rise** in the east?	**Where does** the sun (it) **rise**?

1. Fill in the blanks with the correct words from the box. Change the forms of verbs if necessary.

> work   smoke   make   get up   travel

1. Two and two _____ four.
2. She _____ in a bank.
3. He _____ at seven o'clock every day.
4. Do you _____? It's not good for your health.
5. I _____ very often. Next time I will go to Paris.

2. Complete the sentences in simple present using the words given.

1. You _____ (not / like) chocolate.
2. We often _____ (go) to the movies.
3. She _____ (not / study) at all.
4. _____ (he / go) to New York often?
5. _____ (they / like) spicy food?

👥 Pair Work

Practice these dialogues replacing the underlined words.

> **A:** Do <u>you</u> listen to music every day?
> **B:** Yes, <u>I</u> do. / No, <u>I</u> don't.
>
> **A:** Does <u>he</u> go to work early?
> **B:** Yes, <u>he</u> does. / No, <u>he</u> doesn't.

Reading • A Wise Blind Woman

 Online Practice

1. Think about your daily routine. How do you start your morning?

In a small town, there was a blind woman. She couldn't see, but she was very kind and hard working. Her routine has never changed. She always gets up at 6:30 a.m., takes a shower, and gets dressed. At seven, she has a good breakfast and exercises.

One day, a famous doctor visited her house and said, "I have incredible herbal medicine. If you take it every day, you can see well again." She replied, "I will do whatever I can. And I will pay when I recover my sight."

The doctor brought her medicine every morning, but because she couldn't see, he stole her furniture and decorations one by one! A few months later, she opened her eyes and could see! She looked around and decided that she wouldn't pay the doctor.

So, the doctor and the woman went to court. The judge asked her why she hadn't paid the doctor. She answered, "I promised I would pay him when I could see well. By the way, before I became blind, I could see all of my chairs, vases, tables and other furniture, but now I can only see my white walls." The judge thought for a while then said, "She doesn't have to pay until she is able to see everything well!"

[Reading Skill: Sequencing**]** Go to Page 98.

2. Read the passage. Write *T* for true or *F* for false for each statement.

1. The blind woman always gets up late. _____
2. She took the herbal medicine every day. _____
3. She had to pay the doctor immediately. _____

👥 Group Work

Discuss these questions in a group.
- What is your morning routine like?
- What do you do in the evening?

Listen Up • Do You Want to Go on a Date?

1. Getting Ready What do you think is the best date idea? Pick one.

go to a concert	go out for dinner	go camping	go to a drive-in movie
play extreme sports	go to a sporting event	visit a museum	go to an amusement park

2. Easy Listening Listen to the dialogue and answer the questions.

1. How did the woman get the concert tickets?
   - **a.** She bought them.
   - **b.** She won them.

2. What time does the concert begin?
   - **a.** at 7:00
   - **b.** at 7:30

3. What are they going to do before the concert?
   - **a.** talk over coffee
   - **b.** have lunch

3. Hard Rock Listen to the dialogue and answer the questions.

1. What is the survey about?
   - **a.** the use of technology
   - **b.** current news

2. How many phone calls does the man usually make?
   - **a.** four or five
   - **b.** five or six

4. Pronunciation Third Person Verb Endings
Listen and practice. Notice how the final –s(es) is pronounced.

[s]	She **sleeps** seven hours a day.	Jenny usually **gets** up at 7:30.
[z]	He **plays** soccer on Sundays.	He **reads** every day.
[iz]	He **misses** his parents.	He **watches** TV every night.

• Speaking Build-up • When Do You Usually Exercise?

1. Study how adverbs of frequency are used.

A: When do you usually eat breakfast?
B: Around seven o'clock.
A: Do you always wake up early?
B: No, sometimes I sleep until eight.
A: When do you exercise?
B: I always exercise at night before bedtime.

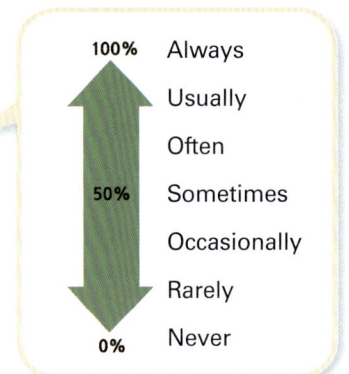

2. When do you do the following activities? Write your answers.

Activities	e.g.) John	You	Your partner
wake up	always at 6:30		
check email	usually in the evening		
take a shower	always at night		
read a book	sometimes after dinner		
exercise	usually in the morning		
go shopping	often on the weekend		
listen to music	always before bed		
eat lunch	usually at 12:30		
watch TV	occasionally after midnight		
go to a concert	never		

Pair Work

Practice this dialogue using the chart above. Write your partner's answers in the chart.

A: What time do you wake up?   B: I usually wake up at 6:30.

Culture Awareness | Expectations of Punctuality

People from other countries and cultures have different expectations of punctuality. Things run on-time in most of America and Europe. In South America, it is common to be 30 minutes to an hour late. So, be aware of the differences and plan ahead. However, it is always good to be 10 minutes early, especially for an interview.

Tips Always plan to be 10 minutes early. People will be happy with what you do.

[Writing: My Daily Routine] Go to Page 99.

Review Units 04~06

• Conversation •   Mango's Big Day

Listen to the conversation and fill in the blanks.

Jerry: Cindy, have you seen Mango today?

Cindy: Isn't he around here? He was here at lunch time.

Jerry: Yes, he was here when I came home for lunch.
We _____ _____ _____ _____ as always.
Now I can't find him anywhere.

Cindy: Oh, look there! Mango's coming. He's a mess. _____
_____ some flowers in his fur.

Jerry: He must have gone near the _____ _____.
We _____ go there _____ _____.
And a lady at the flower shop _____ gives Mango a special treat.

Cindy: I think he must have gone there for the special treat.

Jerry: I think so. But I locked him up after lunch, and I don't know how he got out again.

Cindy: Oh, well. That's a mystery.

👥 Pair Work

Think of the time you were lost or any items you've lost. Then ask and answer about the time or the items with your partner.

• Have you ever been lost?	• Have you ever lost anything?
• When was it? And how were you lost?	• When was it? And how did you lose it?
• Where were you found?	• Did you find it?

Reading • The First Airplane

Read the passage and choose the best answer to each question.

Wilbur and Orville Wright designed, built, and flew the first airplane in 1903. They were born in Dayton, Ohio. In 1896, **they** began to have an interest in gliders. From 1900 to 1902, they designed, built and flew a series of three gliders called the Wright Gliders. In 1900, the Wright brothers tested their first glider near the town of Kitty Hawk, North Carolina. The windy hills were a good place for the gliders to take off. Then they succeeded in flying in their second glider in 1901 and the third in 1902. During that time, they tested many kinds of wings and control systems. After the tests, the Wright brothers decided to design and make an airplane. They planned an airplane like a glider, but it had its own engine. The Wrights made the airplane with a gasoline engine in 1903. It had two propellers. They tested their plane in Kill Devil Hills, near Kitty Hawk. Orville made a success of the first flight in the airplane on December 17, 1903. He flew 37 meters in 12 seconds. Later that day, Wilbur flew 260 meters in 59 seconds.

1. **What is the passage mainly about?**
   a. the history of airplanes
   b. the childhood of the Wright brothers
   c. the differences between gliders and planes
   d. the Wright brothers and the first airplane flight

2. **In the first paragraph, the word "they" refers to _____.**
   a. the airplanes
   b. the gliders
   c. the wings
   d. the Wright brothers

3. **Where did the Wright brothers test their first glider?**
   a. in Kill Devil Hills, near Kitty Hawk
   b. in Dayton, Ohio
   c. near the town of Kitty Hawk
   d. in South Carolina

4. **Which was the farthest distance that the Wright brothers flew their first plane?**
   a. 37 meters
   b. 12 meters
   c. 260 meters
   d. 59 meters

Vocabulary	Conversation	Grammar Point	Reading	Listen Up	Speaking Build-up
Physical Appearance	Wow! He Looks Really Handsome	Order of Adjectives	Queen Yuna	What Do They Look like?	Could You Tell Me about Him?

UNIT 07 He's Tall and Muscular

• Vocabulary • Physical Appearance

1. Study the words below.

  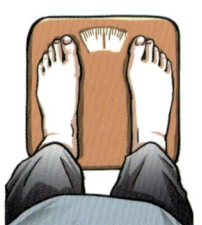  

Age	Height	Weight	Hair	Others
young	short	skinny	blond	handsome
middle-aged	medium height	thin	curly	pretty
old	tall	slim	straight	beautiful
elderly	**Body Shape**	slender	**Skin**	good-looking
child / children	petite	underweight	brown	healthy
teenager	muscular	plump	dark	ugly
adolescent	well-built	stocky	fair	mustache
adult	fit	overweight	pale	beard
			tanned	

2. Fill in the blanks with the correct words from the box.

skinny	medium height	overweight

1. A more polite word for describing someone who is "fat" is _____.
2. The opposite of "fat" is "thin". Another word meaning "thin" is _____.
3. He is not tall or short. He is _____.

 Pair Work

Practice asking and answering about someone's appearance.

A: Does she have curly hair?
B: No, she has straight hair.

A: Is she plump?
B: No, she is slim.

48 CONNECTED 1

Conversation • Wow! He Looks Really Handsome

1. Look at the picture and describe what is happening.

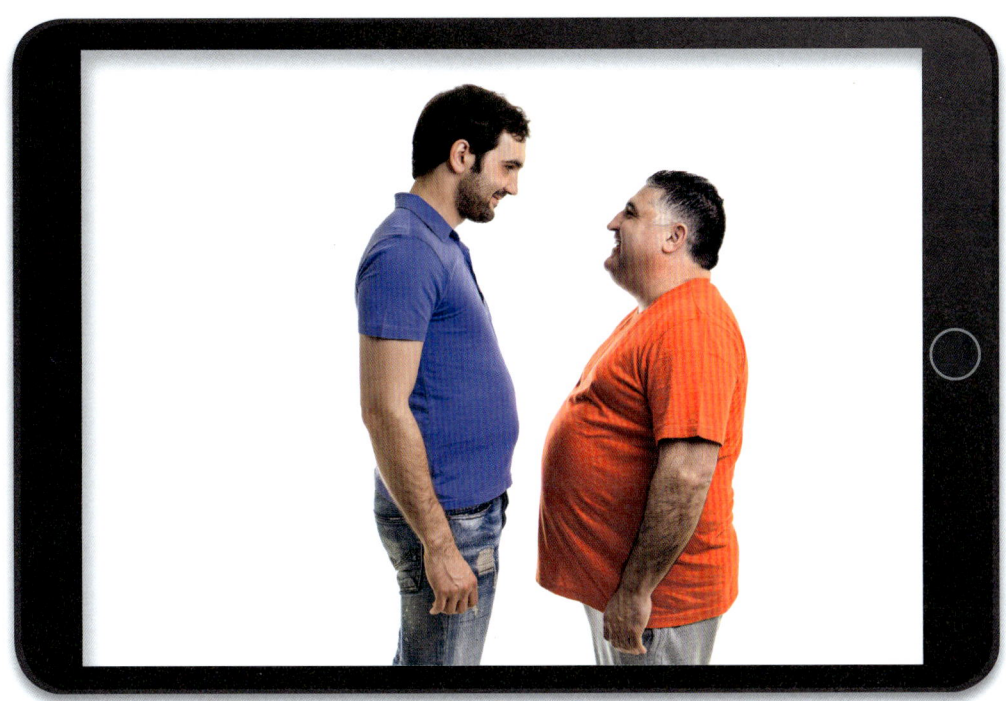

2. Listen to the conversation and fill in the blanks.

Cindy: Kimberly brought her new boyfriend to the party last night.

Annie: Oh, could you tell me about him?

Cindy: Well, actually… He's kind of _____ and a little _____.

Annie: I don't believe it. I thought Kimberly's ideal man was _____, _____ and _____. Not short and round… Okay, then why are they dating?

Cindy: Maybe it's because he's so funny and very _____.

Annie: Really? Maybe he has a brother that might like me?

Cindy: Sorry, no luck there. He has three older sisters.

Pair Work

Ask and answer about what type of people you like.

> **A:** Do you like a <u>tall or short</u> man / woman?
> **B:** I like a <u>tall</u> man / woman.

Unit 07 He's Tall and Muscular 49

Grammar Point — Order of Adjectives

General Opinion	Specific Opinion	Size	Age	Shape	Color	Origin	Material
good	delicious	big	new	round	red	French	wooden
beautiful	friendly	tiny	ancient	square	dark	Chinese	cotton
important	comfortable	small	young	heart	white	Italian	paper

1. Complete the sentences by putting the adjectives in the correct order.

1. He likes that _____ car parked in front of his house.
   (brand-new / compact / blue)
2. Genie has _____ Afghan Hounds.
   (gorgeous / white / ten / big)
3. Michelle has a _____ table.
   (pretty / antique / Italian)
4. There is a _____ dish.
   (small / round / brown)
5. She likes the _____ chair.
   (shiny / metal / gray)

2. Circle the correct words.

1. The chair is not cozy. It is (uncomfortable / comfortable).
2. This cookie is cheap, not (reasonable / expensive).
3. My brother is not fat. He is (fit / full).
4. She is not quiet. She is (talkative / shy).
5. It is too bright to open my eyes. I hope it is a little (dark / light).

Pair Work

Practice this dialogue replacing the underlined words.

A: What does the lamp look like?
B: It's a tiny square white lamp.

Reading • Queen Yuna

1. Think about how important physical appearance is in one's life.

Yuna Kim is a world famous figure skater. She is slim and of average height. She has long, slim arms and legs. She has brown eyes and brown hair. Her lower body, from the waist to the anklebone, measures 96 cm, which is almost double her torso. She is considered long-legged, and because of her long legs, her jumps look bigger and more elegant.

She is the 2010 Olympic champion and the 2014 Olympic silver medalist in ladies' single figure skating. She is also the 2009 and 2013 World champion and the 2009 Four Continents champion. Kim is the first Korean figure skater to win a medal at an ISU Junior or Senior Grand Prix event, an ISU Championship, and the Olympic Games. She is the first female skater to achieve a "grand slam" of four major championships: the Olympic Games, the World Championships, the Four Continents Championships, and the Grand Prix Final. She is one of the most highly recognized athletes in South Korea. She is called "Queen Yuna" by various media across the world.

She has broken world records eleven times since 2007. She is the first female skater to surpass the 200-point total mark. During the Vancouver Olympics in 2010, she surprised the world by scoring 228.56 points.

[Reading Skill: Scanning for Details] Go to Page 100.

2. Read the passage and answer the following questions.

1. **What is NOT true about Yuna Kim?**
   a. She broke world records 11 times.
   b. She is the 2010 Olympic champion.
   c. She was the world champion in 2008.
   d. She is the first female skater to win a grand slam.

2. **Which does NOT belong to the grand slam championship of figure skating?**
   a. the Olympic Games
   b. the ISU Championship
   c. the World Championships
   d. the Four Continents Championships

Group Work

Discuss these questions in a group.
- What is the first thing you notice about a person?
- Is there a part of your appearance that you are very proud of?

• **Listen Up** • **What Do They Look like?**

1. Getting Ready Listen to each description and write the letter on the correct picture.

1.   2.   3.   4.

2. Easy Listening Listen to the dialogue and answer the questions.

1. What are the women talking about?
   a. how Mary's blind date was
   b. what Mary's ideal type looks like

2. What does Mary's date look like?
   a. average height and weight
   b. average height and green eyes

3. Hard Rock Listen to the news broadcast and answer the questions.

1. What does the man look like?
   a. slender and tall
   b. strong and healthy

2. The man's eyes are _____ and the woman's eyes are _____.
   a. blue – brown
   b. blue – green

3. Why are they considered dangerous?
   a. They carry weapons.
   b. They have long arms.

4. Pronunciation Linking Sounds: [z] and [ʃ]

Listen and practice. Notice the linking sounds of [z] and [ʃ] in the sentences.

• Speaking Build-up • Could You Tell Me about Him?

1. Study the expressions for describing appearance.

A: How old is he?
B: He's in his late teens.
A: What does he look like?
B: He's average height and slim as a reed.
A: What kind of hair does he have?
B: He has short spiky black hair.
A: What kind of person is he?
B: He is very kind and funny.

age
- in his teens / twenties / thirties / etc.
- He's very young.
- mature / old / a senior citizen

hair
- graying hair
- thick / bushy hair
- curly / wavy hair
- bald

2. Complete the chart describing the following people.

	Age	Appearance	Hair style	Personality
e.g.) **Sean**	in his early twenties	average height and a little plump	short curly brown hair	quiet and friendly
Your best friend				
Your favorite actor / actress				

Pair Work
Practice the dialogue in Part 1 using the chart above.

Culture Awareness — Beauty Is in the Eye of the Beholder

Beauty is in the eye of the beholder. What one person finds attractive may not appeal to someone else. Every country and culture has its own standard of what it considers beautiful. For some, it may be big eyes and a long neck. Others may find a round face more attractive. Some people try to augment their bodies with tattoos, piercings, or scars. They may not appeal to you, but to them they look gorgeous. As you can generalize, it is easier to say that no two people have exactly the same standard of beauty.

[Writing: What Makes You Like Someone?] Go to Page 101.

UNIT 08 What Are You Doing?

| Vocabulary
Free Time Activities | Conversation
What Do You Do
In Your Free Time? | Grammar Point
Present Progressive | Reading
Kelly's Family
on a Weekend | Listen Up
Do You Want to
Learn Something New? | Speaking Build-up
Would You Like to
Take a Walk? |

Vocabulary • Free Time Activities

1. Choose the correct word for each picture and write the letter.

| a. clean the room | b. play computer games | c. play the guitar | d. work out |
| e. cook dinner | f. take a walk | g. meet friends | h. study |

2. Fill in the blanks with the correct words from the box above. Change the forms of the verbs if necessary.

1. Why don't you _____? Your bed is messy, and the floor is dirty.
2. She is _____ for her family. They all love her food.
3. Do you _____ at the gym every day?

 Pair Work

Practice this dialogue replacing the underlined words.

> **A:** What are you doing?
> **B:** I'm <u>cooking dinner for my family</u>.

54 CONNECTED 1

• **Conversation** • **What Do You Do in Your Free Time?**

1. Look at the picture and describe what is happening.

2. Listen to the conversation and fill in the blanks.

Andy: What are you up to?

Brad: I'm learning to _____ _____ _____.

Andy: Why are you learning to play the guitar?

Brad: I'm trying to get Jennifer to go out with me. She said she likes musicians.

Andy: I see. By the way, I thought we were going to _____ _____ _____ and _____ _____.

Brad: Sorry, I lost track of time. Shall we _____ _____ _____ or get a taxi to the restaurant?

Andy: It's still early. We can walk.

Pair Work

Ask and answer about your free time activities.

> **A:** What do you usually do in your free time?
> **B:** I usually play the guitar.

Unit 08 What Are You Doing? 55

Grammar Point • Present Progressive

Form: **Be verb** + Verb-**ing**

Statements		Questions
Affirmative	**Negative**	
I **am** cook**ing**.	*I* **am not** cook**ing**.	**Am** *I* cook**ing**?
You **are** study**ing**.	*You* **are not** study**ing**.	**Are** *you* study**ing**?
He/She/It **is** work**ing**.	*He/She/It* **is** not work**ing**.	**Is** *he/she/it* work**ing**?
You/We/They **are** sing**ing**.	*You/We/They* **are** not sing**ing**.	**Are** *you/we/they* sing**ing**?

1. Complete the sentences in present progressive using the words given.

1. Jonathan _____ (sleep) on the beach.
2. Mindy and Sally _____ (discuss) the issue.
3. I _____ (talk) to Jake about the party.
4. She _____ (not / help) the disabled man.
5. My parents do not drink coffee, so they _____ (have) tea.

2. Look for grammatical errors. Rewrite the sentences correctly in present progressive.

1. I am pray in the church.
2. Does she speaking in English right now?
3. Is you doing your homework?
4. They are not talk about the books.
5. Does he eating pasta now?

Pair Work

Practice this dialogue replacing the underlined words.

A: <u>Are they watching a movie?</u>
B: Yes, <u>they are</u>. / No, <u>they're</u> not. <u>They're doing their homework.</u>

• **Reading** • **Kelly's Family on a Weekend**

1. Think about what you and your family do on weekends.

It's a stormy Saturday. It's raining heavily, and Kelly and her family are spending the afternoon at home. Kelly and her father are in the living room. Kelly is working on an assignment for her art class. Her father, Mr. Harris, is surfing the Internet to buy a new tool kit. Kelly's older brother, Peter, is in his bedroom playing computer games. He spends a lot of time on the computer. He always says he will be like Bill Gates. Kelly's mother, Mrs. Harris, is in the kitchen preparing a snack for everyone. All of them love Fluffy, the family cat. He is sleeping on the sofa in the living room. Fluffy loves to play with a toy mouse.

[**Reading Skill:** Skimming] Go to Page 102.

2. Read the passage and answer the following questions.

1. What day of the week is it?
2. Where is Kelly?
3. What is Kelly doing?
4. What is Mr. Harris doing?
5. What is Mrs. Harris preparing in the kitchen?

Group Work

Discuss these questions in a group.

- What do you usually do on weekends?
- How do you usually spend time with your family?

• **Listen Up** • **Do You Want to Learn Something New?**

1. **Getting Ready** Listen to each statement and write the letter on the correct picture.

1.
2.
3.
4.

2. **Easy Listening** Listen to the dialogue and answer the questions.

1. **What is the woman doing?**
   a. She is checking the mattress.
   b. She is tossing and turning.

2. **What is the reason she needs to change the mattress?**
   a. There are bedbugs in the mattress.
   b. There are dirty spots in the mattress.

3. **Hard Rock** Listen to the advertisement and answer the questions.

1. **Where can you find a list of classes that are available?**
   a. on the telephone
   b. at the community center

2. **What kinds of classes are NOT available at the community center?**
   a. art classes
   b. language classes

4. **Pronunciation** Rising and Falling Intonation

Listen and practice. Notice the rising and falling intonation at the end of the sentences.

Rising Intonation	Falling Intonation
Is it five o'clock yet? ↗	What time is it? ↘
Is he coming? ↗	When is he coming? ↘
What did you just say? ↗	Write your name. ↘
What did you say your name was? ↗	The color is blue. ↘

Rising Intonation: Yes-No questions and wh-questions for clarification or restatement

Falling Intonation: Wh-questions, commands, and statements with a period

• Speaking Build-up • Would You Like to Take a Walk?

1. Study the expressions for making suggestions.

A: What do you want to do?
B: How about taking a walk?
A: It's too hot today.
B: Then we could go swimming.
A: Sorry, I don't like swimming.
B: How about going to see a movie?
A: A movie and air conditioning. Yes!

A
- Would you like to...?
- What would you like to do?

B
- Why don't we + *verb*...?
- Would you like to...?
- Let's + verb...

2. Choose one activity that you'd like to do in each of the following weather conditions. Write down your answers.

build a snowman, have a snowball fight, go swimming, go snorkeling, play volleyball, go for a hike, go for a ride, go on a picnic, watch a movie, read a book, draw a picture, play a board game

Weather conditions	What you want to do	What your partner wants to do
on a rainy day		
on a cold and snowy day		
on a sunny day		
on a hot and humid day		

Pair Work Practice this dialogue using your answers above. Then complete the chart with your partner's answers.

A: It's rainy today. What would you like to do?
B: I'd like to play a board game.

Culture Awareness — Is Watching TV a Hobby?

Most Westerners take time out of their schedule to do special activities. Many of them find time to take up a new activity. Some people turn their weekend activity into a new profession. While sitting around the house and watching TV can be fun, it is not a hobby. For a hobby to be a true hobby, it requires a little energy from the person to complete it.

[Writing: What Is Your Favorite Free Time Activity?] Go to Page 103.

UNIT 09

Vocabulary	Conversation	Grammar Point	Reading	Listen Up	Speaking Build-up
Adjectives for Making Comparisons	Is This One Better than That One?	Comparatives / Superlatives	Prague, One of the Most Popular Cities in the World	It's the Most Amazing Thing	I Think the Yellow One Is the Best

Which One Is Prettier?

• Vocabulary • Adjectives for Making Comparisons

 Online Practice

1. Choose and write the correct pair of words for each pair of pictures.

> cheap - expensive   tight - loose   quiet - talkative   picky - easygoing   generous - mean

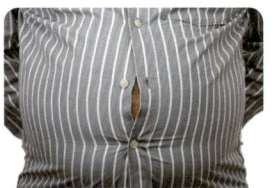   

_____ & _____   _____ & _____

_____ & _____   _____ & _____

2. Fill in the blanks with the correct words from the box above.

1. He was _____ enough to forgive me.
2. **A:** Other pens are seven dollars, but this one is ten.
   B: How come this pen is more _____?
3. It's too _____. Do you have a little bit larger size?

 Pair Work

Practice making comparisons replacing the underlined words.

> **A:** Which one do you like more?
> **B:** I like the <u>tight one</u> better.

60   CONNECTED 1

• Conversation • **Is This One Better than That One?**

1. Look at the picture and describe what is happening.

2. Listen to the conversation and fill in the blanks.

Shannon: Rachel, what do you think about this blouse?

Rachel: It's nice, Shannon. But this one's _____.

Shannon: Wow, look at the price! It's _____ _____ _____ blouse here.

Rachel: But I think none of these look _____ than this one.

I want to buy it, but I can't. I don't have enough money.

Shannon: Well, let me buy it for you.

Rachel: You are _____ _____ _____ person I know. But, I …

Shannon: Your birthday is in a few weeks… It's an early present.

Rachel: Oh, thank you!

Shannon: You're welcome.

Pair Work

Ask and answer questions about comparing clothing items.

A: Do you think this <u>dress</u> is <u>prettier</u> than that one?
B: Yes, I think so. / No, that one is much <u>prettier</u>.

• Grammar Point • Comparatives / Superlatives

	Adjectives	Comparatives	Superlatives
Add –er / –est	cheap picky	cheap<u>er</u> pick<u>ier</u>	cheap<u>est</u> pick<u>iest</u>
Add **more…** / **most…**	expensive	<u>more</u> expensive	<u>most</u> expensive
Irregular forms	good bad many little far	better worse more less farther / further	best worst most least farthest / furthest

1. Circle the correct words.

1. His piece of cake is (big / bigger / biggest) than mine.
2. Everyone knows that Marcie is the (smart / smarter / smartest) in the class.
3. My brother is (strong / stronger / strongest) than me.
4. Our homework last night was (easy / easier / easiest).
5. The Antarctic is the (cold / coder / coldest) place on earth.

2. Choose the correct answers to complete the sentences.

1. I think Marilyn Monroe was _____ Madonna.
   a. more beautiful than   **b.** beautifuller than   **c.** more beautifuller than   **d.** more beautiful as
2. A bike is _____ a car.
   a. more cheap than   **b.** cheaper than   **c.** more cheaper than   **d.** cheaper as
3. When it came to math, Phillip was _____ student in the class.
   a. the worst   **b.** worst   **c.** the most bad   **d.** the baddest
4. CDs are much _____ tapes, and nobody listens to tapes anymore.
   a. more moderner than   **b.** moderner than   **c.** more modern than   **d.** more modern as
5. This is the _____ house in the town.
   a. most expensive   **b.** expensiver   **c.** expensivest   **d.** more expensive

 Pair Work Practice making comparisons replacing the underlined words.

> **A:** Which <u>subject</u> is <u>easier</u>?   **B:** I think <u>science</u> is <u>easier than English</u>.

Reading • Prague, One of the Most Popular Cities in the World

1. Think about the cities in the world you've visited or you want to visit.

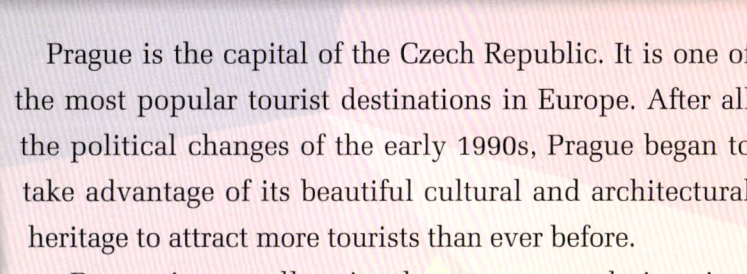

Prague is the capital of the Czech Republic. It is one of the most popular tourist destinations in Europe. After all the political changes of the early 1990s, Prague began to take advantage of its beautiful cultural and architectural heritage to attract more tourists than ever before.

Prague is a smaller city than many people imagine, and it is very easy to move around this wonderful city on foot. Public transportation is cheaper in Prague than in most other European cities, but it is often better to walk. That way, you can appreciate the marvelous buildings. If you sit on a bus or a tram, you might miss them. The Prague Castle is an especially beautiful area located on the mountain. It has a beautiful view of the city and great churches.

Few people leave the city of Prague without commenting on the superb food and drink available. Eating out in Prague is a little expensive, but you can still have a three-course meal for around $15 without any problems.

[**Reading Skill:** Identifying the Topic and Main Idea] Go to Page 104.

2. Read the passage and answer the following questions.

1. What is the story mainly about?
   - a. the beautiful culture in Prague
   - b. Prague in the Czech Republic
   - c. an architectural heritage
   - d. the food of Prague

2. What is the transportation like in Prague?
   - a. It is cheaper than most other European cities.
   - b. It is the cheapest in Europe.
   - c. It is more expensive than other European cities.
   - d. It is the most expensive in Europe.

3. What is the most beautiful area in Prague?
   - a. Charles Bridge
   - b. Old Town Hall
   - c. Astronomical Clock
   - d. Praha Castle

 Group Work

Discuss these questions in a group.
- What city or country do you think is the most beautiful in the world?
- What city or country would you like to live in the most?

• **Listen Up** • It's the Most Amazing Thing

1. Getting Ready Listen to each statement and write the letter on the correct picture.

1.
2.
3.
4.

2. Easy Listening Listen to the dialogue and answer the questions.

1. What are the two women talking about?
   a. a person
   b. their food preference

2. What kind of food does Matthew eat?
   a. only vegetables
   b. only meat

3. Why is Sarah curious about Matthew?
   a. He's the new employee.
   b. She has a date with him.

3. Hard Rock Listen to the dialogue and answer the questions.

1. What is one way to save money when buying house items?
   a. buying them in bulk
   b. asking for a discount

2. Why would it be unwise to buy things in bulk?
   a. because they are expensive
   b. because it could be a waste of money

4. Pronunciation Vowel Sounds: [iː], [e], and [ɪ]

Listen and practice. Notice the different sounds of [iː], [e], and [ɪ] in the words.

[iː]	[e]	[ɪ]
feel	fell	fill
beat	bet	bit
reed	red	rid

• Speaking Build-up • I Think the Yellow One Is the Best

1. Study the expressions for clothes shopping.

A: What do you think about that shirt?
B: Try that on. See if it fits.
A: Maybe this one will be better… It's smaller.
Ah, no. It's too small.
B: What about this one? It's bigger.
A: Nope, this one is too big.
B: Let's find one that fits you. Well… This one might work.
A: Okay. Let me try it on.

B
- Try this on for size.
- See if this one fits.

A
- This one might work.
- Perhaps this will work.

2. Complete the chart by writing sentences to compare the three objects in each group.

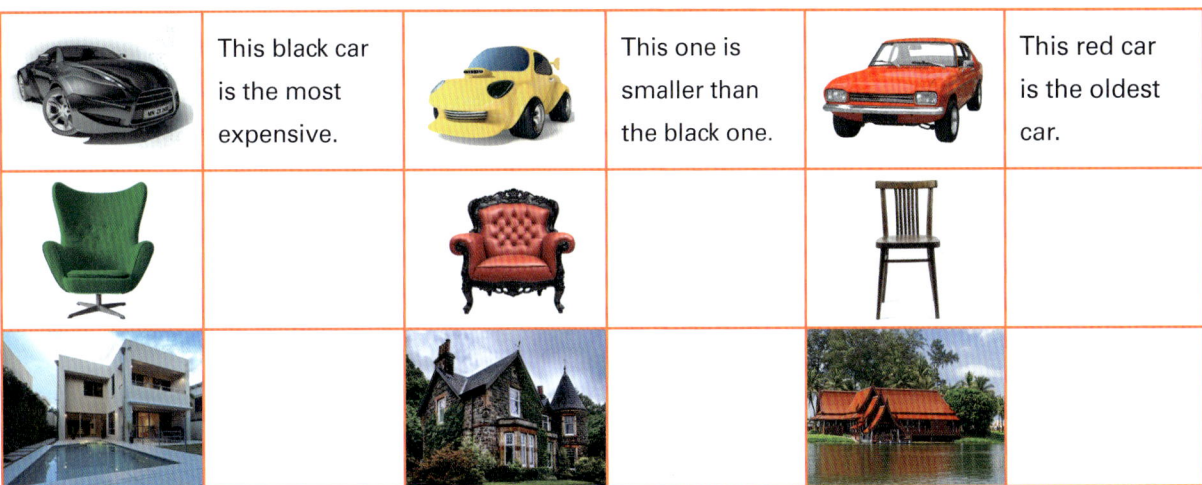

	This black car is the most expensive.		This one is smaller than the black one.		This red car is the oldest car.

Pair Work

Practice this dialogue using the chart above.

A: I think the black car is the most amazing.
B: Really? I think the red one is better.
A: But the black one is the most expensive.
B: True, but the red color is much better.

Culture Awareness — How Tight Is Too Tight?

Different places around the world have different standards of what fits. In America, the trend for clothes is to wear them loose and comfortable. In Brazil, it is the opposite. Many of them want clothes to be as tight as possible. Some people like their clothes to be skin-tight with little or no extra room, but others like baggy and comfortable clothes. It is all a matter of your personal preference.

[Writing: Which One Do You Like More?] Go to Page 105.

Review Units 07~09

• Conversation •   Shopping on Rodeo Dr.

Listen to the conversation and fill in the blanks.

Shannon: Wow, Annie, _____ _____ on Rodeo Dr.
Annie: I know some of the stores here are the _____ _____ stores in the world.
Shannon: What do you _____ _____ _____ for?
Annie: I don't know. Hey, look at the couple who are walking toward us. Isn't that Brad and Angelina?
Shannon: No way. Brad's _____ and _____ _____… And Angelina is a lot _____.
Annie: I guess you're right. But they did look like them… a little…
Shannon: No, they didn't! Are you feeling okay?
Annie: It's just a little hot. _____ _____ we go get something cool to drink?
Shannon: Sounds good.
Annie: And let's _____ _____ _____ after that. Maybe we'll see another famous face.

 Pair Work

Play a guessing game following the steps below.

GUESS WHO?

1. Choose one classmate in your mind.
2. Have your partner ask six *yes* or *no* questions about the person's appearance. Let him/her guess who the person is by asking questions like the ones below. Answer your partner's questions with *yes* or *no*.

   > Is it a man? / Is it a woman? / Does she have long hair? / Is she tall? / Is she slender? / Is it Rachel?

3. Switch roles.

Reading • Who Was Cleopatra?

Read the passage and choose the best answer to each question.

Have you heard of Cleopatra? Cleopatra was a woman who ruled Egypt during the time of the powerful Roman Empire as a queen. Egypt is a country in Africa known for its big pyramids. There are numerous legends about Cleopatra. Cleopatra spoke many languages and was a very strong queen. Under her rule, Egypt became much richer. According to some stories, she was a great beauty whom men could not resist. You may say Cleopatra is not prettier than modern beauties because her make-up is so strong.

In other stories, she is described as so hungry for power that she killed her own brothers and sister. When Cleopatra was 18 years old, she became queen of all Egypt. In the beginning, she ruled the country with one of her brothers. But later on, she went to war against him. It was a difficult battle, but she won!

Cleopatra's rule as queen only ended after Egypt was attacked by Rome. Her army was not as strong as the mighty Romans. Soon after Egypt was defeated, Cleopatra died. Nobody is exactly sure how it happened. Many believe that she killed herself by letting a poisonous snake bite her. Yet the legend about the attractive beauty who dealt with some of the most powerful men continues to survive.

1. **Cleopatra was a queen of _____.**
   a. Africa b. Egypt c. Rome d. Italy

2. **Cleopatra became queen at the age of _____.**
   a. 15 b. 18 c. 20 d. 30

3. **What kind of queen was Cleopatra?**
   a. weak b. generous c. strong d. warm-hearted

4. **Modern people may NOT think she _____.**
   a. was prettier than modern beauties
   b. had strong make-up
   c. was richer than her brothers
   d. was smarter than modern people

5. **How did Cleopatra die?**
   a. in a fire b. of a snake bite c. with poison d. Nobody knows for sure.

Vocabulary	Conversation	Grammar Point	Reading	Listen Up	Speaking Build-up
Past Events	What Happened Last Night?	Simple Past	The Egyptian Classes and Occupations	Where Were They at That Time?	Did You Do Anything Special?

UNIT 10

What Did You Do This Morning?

• Vocabulary • Past Events

1. Complete the sentences with the correct words from the box. Use the past forms of the verbs.

| drive a car | get a haircut | take pictures |
| take a bus | see a doctor | hang out with friends |

1.
Julia _____ to work this morning.

2. Selena _____ this morning.

3.
Greg _____ yesterday.

4.
Cindy _____ a few days ago.

5.
Samantha _____ in the park last Sunday.

6.
Jade _____ to school this morning.

 Pair Work

Practice this dialogue replacing the underlined words.

A: Did you <u>see a doctor</u> yesterday?
B: Yes, I did. / No, I didn't.

68 CONNECTED 1

• **Conversation** • **What Happened Last Night?**

1. Look at the picture and describe what is happening.

2. Listen to the conversation and fill in the blanks.

Lilly: Hey, James. What's wrong?

James: My car has a flat tire.

Lilly: What happened? What _____ _____ _____?

James: I don't know. I _____ _____ a shopping mall with John yesterday afternoon.

Lilly: Did your car have a flat tire there?

James: I don't think so. It _____ _____ when I was driving to John's house after shopping.

Lilly: Did you go through any construction zone?

James: Oh, yes… Maybe my car had a flat there.

Lilly: Did you fix your car?

James: No, not yet. I just _____ it at John's house.

Pair Work

Ask and answer about what you did over the weekend.

A: What did you do on Saturday afternoon?
B: I went shopping at the mall.

Grammar Point • Simple Past

Online Practice

Present Verb Forms	Past Verb Forms		Simple Past	
	Affirmative	Negative	Statements	Questions
am / is are	was were	wasn't weren't	I **was** happy. They **weren't** tired.	**Was** she **happy**? **Were** they **tired**?
call wash visit	called washed visited	didn't call didn't wash didn't visit	I **called** you last night. She **didn't wash** the car. They **visited** my mother.	**Did** you **call** me? What **did** she **wash**? **Did** they **visit** my mother?
take see	took saw	didn't take didn't see	We **didn't take** a taxi. They **saw** the house.	**Did** we **take** a taxi? What **did** they **see**?

1. Fill in the blanks with the correct words.

1. **A:** Where did you go on holiday? **B:** I _____ to Spain.
2. **A:** How was the party? **B:** It _____ great.
3. **A:** Where did you visit yesterday? **B:** I _____ an art museum.
4. **A:** Who were you with in the park? **B:** I _____ with two friends of mine.
5. **A:** What did you buy for your mother? **B:** I _____ a scarf.

2. Unscramble the words and complete the sentences in simple past.

1. the bus / miss / Janet / . _____
2. She / her room / tidy / . _____
3. Nancy / the concert / not / to / go / . _____
4. by the river / see / many birds / They / . _____
5. do / He / after dinner / the dishes / not / . _____

Pair Work

Ask and answer about what you did last night.

A: What did you do last night?
B: I hung out with friends.

Reading • The Egyptian Classes and Occupations

1. What do you know about Egypt? Think about what ancient Egypt was like.

Most ancient societies were divided into two groups: the "haves" and the "have-nots." The "haves" were the upper classes. They were generally rulers, nobles, and priests. The "have-nots" were mostly merchants, artists, and farmers. Although merchants and artists were considered better than peasants, they were still lower than nobles and priests. In every ancient civilization, there was a large slave class at the bottom.

In ancient Egypt, there were four social classes. At the top there was the royal family. They were a large number of nobles and priests. In the next class, there were professional soldiers and scribes (record-keepers). The next were the farmers. Some farmers worked in cities, others worked in mines. At the bottom, of course, there were the slaves. Many of them were brought to Egypt as prisoners of war. Other slaves were people who sold themselves because of debt or foreigners who wanted to become an Egyptian.

The ruler of ancient Egypt was the pharaoh, a name that meant "a great house." The pharaoh had great power and was believed to be a god on Earth.

[**Reading Skill:** Finding Supporting Details] Go to Page 106.

2. Read the passage and answer the following questions.

1. Who did NOT belong to the upper classes in most ancient societies?
   - **a.** rulers
   - **b.** nobles
   - **c.** artists
   - **d.** priests

2. How many social classes were there in ancient Egypt?
   - **a.** two
   - **b.** three
   - **c.** four
   - **d.** five

3. Who were in the third class of ancient Egypt?
   - **a.** royal family members
   - **b.** professional soldiers
   - **c.** scribes
   - **d.** farmers

Group Work

Discuss these questions in a group.
- Is there any country you find interesting?
- What is so special about the country?

• Listen Up • **Where Were They at That Time?**

1. Getting Ready Listen and circle the correct words.

Yesterday it **(was windy / windy)** in the afternoon. I **(sat / sit)** on the bench in the park. Suddenly it **(was started / started)** to rain, and a strong wind **(was blown / blew)** my umbrella inside out.

2. Easy Listening Listen to Chris's story and answer the questions.

1. What was Chris doing in Toronto in 2005?
   a. studying at a college
   b. teaching at a college

2. Where was he last month, and what was he doing there?
   a. in Toronto, studying
   b. in Vienna, playing the piano

3. Hard Rock Listen to the dialogue and answer the questions.

1. When did the woman last visit a museum?
   a. three months ago
   b. eight months ago

2. What part of her body did she break?
   a. her leg
   b. her nose

3. What did she do last week?
   a. read a book
   b. got a haircut

4. Pronunciation Final -ed(-d) of Regular Past Verbs
Listen and practice. Notice the final sounds of [d], [ɪd], and [t] in past verb forms.

[d]	[ɪd]	[t]
lov**ed**	visit**ed**	watch**ed**
bang**ed**	edit**ed**	popp**ed**
stay**ed**	land**ed**	cook**ed**

Speaking Build-up • Did You Do Anything Special?

1. Study the expressions to ask about what you did.

A: How was the weekend? Did you have fun?
B: Not really. I had to do my laundry.
A: Really? Mine was an adventure.
B: Oh, what did you do?
A: I finished an epic novel about thrones.

A
- How was yesterday?
- What did you do last night?
- Did anything special happen yesterday?

2. Put checks (√) in the correct blank spaces based on the activities you did.

	You			Your partner		
	Last month	Last week	Yesterday	Last month	Last week	Yesterday
see a movie						
do homework						
take pictures						
get a haircut						
go shopping						
cook dinner						
see a doctor						
study English						

Pair Work Ask and answer questions about the activities in the chart above. Write your partner's answers in the chart.

A: When did you see a movie?
B: I saw a movie last month. How about you?
A: I saw one last week.

Culture Awareness — I'll Do It Later

*Procrastination - Is a sin, that only leads to sorrow. I can give it up at any time.
I think I will... Tomorrow.*   -Anonymous

We all have things we need to get done in life. Sometimes it is a matter of putting which is most important first. Don't forget to take some time for yourself once in a while. Relax and don't panic.

[Writing: What a Weekend!] Go to Page 107.

UNIT 11 I Can Play Tennis

Vocabulary	Conversation	Grammar Point	Reading	Listen Up	Speaking Build-up
Hobbies and Abilities	I Love Playing Tennis	*Can* for Ability	Soccer Is Popular	Let's Go See a Game	Are You Good at Playing Soccer?

Vocabulary • Hobbies and Abilities

 Online Practice

1. Choose the correct words for each picture and write the letter.

a. play the trumpet	b. play baseball	c. play the violin
d. play tennis	e. play soccer	f. ski
g. play golf	h. play ice hockey	i. play basketball	j. fence

1.
2.
3.
4.
5.

6.
7.
8.
9.
10.

2. Fill in the blanks using the correct words from the box above.

1. I _____ on Friday afternoons. I take a racket and some balls to the court to play it.
2. He likes to _____ on the weekend because he feels excited about hitting balls into holes on grassy lands.
3. She can _____ very well. She practices shooting the ball on the grass field every day.

Pair Work

Ask and answer about your abilities replacing the underlined words.

A: Can you <u>play tennis</u>?
B: Yes, I can. / No, I can't.

• Conversation • **I Love Playing Tennis**

1. Look at the picture and describe what is happening.

2. Listen to the conversation and fill in the blanks.

Mina: Josh, you are a sportsaholic.
Josh: Why do you think so? I just love playing tennis with you.
Mina: Okay, but what else do you play? Let's see, you play _____ on Mondays and Thursdays.
Josh: Yeah, and _____ on Saturdays.
Mina: Oh, and you go _____ almost every Sunday.
Josh: What can I say? I love sports.
Mina: And that's just summer sports. In winter, you do even more…
Josh: I know I love snowboarding, ice skating, _____, and so much more. They're great.
Mina: I know you do. It's just too bad you're not good at any of them.
Josh: Ouch, that hurts.

Pair Work

Practice this dialogue replacing the underlined words.

A: Let's play the new computer game!
B: Sure, I'm good at computer games. / I'd love to, but I'm not good at computer games.

Grammar Point • *Can* for Ability

Statements		Questions
Affirmative	**Negative**	
I **can** play tennis.	I **cannot**(=**can't**) play tennis.	**Can** you play tennis? What sports **can** you play?

1. Circle the correct words.

1. (Could / Can / Could has) you understand what he is talking about?
2. My sister (can / can to / will) play tennis, but I can't.
3. I (could not / could / have can) walk when I was less than a year old.
4. (Can / Can do / Will have) you tell me what time it is, please?
5. My grandfather (can / could / was able to) walk without any help now.

2. Choose the correct answers to complete the sentences.

1. _____ play the violin?
   a. Do you can   b. Can you   c. Do you be able to   d. Can you do

2. I _____ skiing because I am too tired.
   a. can't to go   b. can go   c. can't go   d. couldn't to go

3. A: What _____ Gina play at the sports day? B: She _____ play basketball.
   a. can   b. is able to   c. do   d. is

4. My uncle _____ golf because he hurt his arms.
   a. can't to play   b. can play   c. can't play   d. can played

5. They _____ English, but they can't write it well.
   a. to speak   b. speaking   c. can speak   d. can't speak

Pair Work

Practice this dialogue replacing the underlined words.

A: What languages can you <u>speak</u>?
B: I can <u>speak English and Chinese</u>.

• Reading • Soccer Is Popular

1. What kind of sports do you like and enjoy playing?

For centuries, people have been playing kicking games with a ball. The game of soccer developed from some of these early games. The English probably gave soccer its name and its first set of rules. In European countries, soccer is called football or association football. Some people believe that the name "soccer" came from "assoc.", an abbreviation for the word association. Others believe that the name came from the high socks that the players wear. Organized soccer games began in 1863.

In soccer, two teams of eleven players try to kick or headbutt the ball into their opponents' goal. The goalie, who tries to keep the ball out of the goal, is the only player on the field who is allowed to touch the ball with his or her hands. The other players must use their feet, heads, and bodies to control the ball.

The most widely watched soccer game is the World Cup. The World Cup, an international soccer competition, has been held every four years since 1930. In the World Cup, 32 national teams from around the world compete for the tournament title over a month. Brazil has won the World Cup tournament five times. Italy and Germany have won four times each. Many people around the world wait for the World Cup season to see which county wins the world championship.

[Reading Skill: Facts and Opinions] Go to Page 108.

2. Read the passage and answer the following questions.

1. Who probably gave soccer its name?
   - a. English people
   - b. Americans
   - c. Brazilians
   - d. Asians

2. What do Europeans call soccer?
   - a. soccer
   - b. football or association football
   - c. assoc.
   - d. European association

3. Which is NOT true about soccer games?
   - a. Each team has 11 players.
   - b. The goalie can touch the ball with his or her hands.
   - c. Organized soccer games started in the mid-1800s.
   - d. Most of world soccer competitions are held in Europe.

👥 Group Work

Discuss this question in a group.

- Which is more important, "what you can do" or "what you want to do"?

• **Listen Up** • Let's Go See a Game

1. **Getting Ready** Listen to each statement and write the letter on the correct picture.

1.
2.
3.
4.

2. **Easy Listening** Listen to the dialogue and answer the questions.

1. What are the two young men trying to watch?
   a. a soccer game
   b. a baseball program

2. What is wrong with the television schedule?
   a. It's for next week.
   b. It's from last week.

3. **Hard Rock** Listen to the dialogue and answer the questions.

1. What is the woman planning to do this weekend?
   a. practice her basketball shot
   b. practice her music

2. What is NOT one of the instruments the woman can play?
   a. the viola
   b. the trumpet

3. What sport can the man play?
   a. basketball
   b. golf

4. **Pronunciation** Voiceless and Voiced Pair: [f] – [v]
Listen and practice. Notice the difference between the [f] sound and the [v] sound in the words.

[f]	**f**ive	**f**ast	**f**riends	ele**ph**ants
[v]	**v**ery	**v**iolent	**v**acuum	ha**v**e

five **v**ery ele**ph**ants **v**iolent **f**riends

78   CONNECTED 1

Speaking Build-up • Are You Good at Playing Soccer?

1. Study the expressions to talk about one's ability.

A: Would you like to play baseball with me?
B: Sure. Do you know how to play?
A: I can play baseball better than you.
B: Really? Are you that good?

B
- Are you able to…?
- How good are you at *verb-ing*…?
- Are you any good at *verb-ing*…?

A: Yes, I play like DiMaggio. How about you?
B: I am better than DiMaggio.
A: Okay, prove it!

A
- I can play better than…
- I am the best at *verb-ing*.
- Yes, I am very good at *verb-ing*…

2. Complete the chart by writing down how well you can do the activities. Try to use the expressions in Part 1.

Activities	e.g.) James	You
play ball games	I can play soccer better than David Beckham.	
dance	I can barely make it around the floor.	
drive a car	I can drive like Mario Andretti.	
swim	I can swim, but only the doggy paddle.	
run a marathon	I can, but not very well.	

Pair Work Ask and answer about how well you can do the activities in the chart above.

A: Do you know how to drive a car?
B: Of course, I'm very good at driving.

Culture Awareness — Sports Days

In some places in the world, coworkers get together in their free time and play a team sport. In Korea, many people like to play volleyball or foot-volleyball. In America, you might be asked to join in for softball or baseball. No matter where you are, people will get together and play sports.

[Writing: What's Your Favorite Sport?] Go to Page 109.

UNIT 12

Vocabulary	Conversation	Grammar Point	Reading	Listen Up	Speaking Build-up
Future Plans	Do You Have Any Plans for Next Year?	Future with *Will*	Robots	It's My Plan!	What Are You Planning to Do?

What Will You Do Next Year?

• Vocabulary • Future Plans

 Online Practice

1. Choose the correct word for the picture in each bubble and write the letter.

a. travel

b. go on a date

c. go on a diet

d. learn the cello

e. graduate from college

f. get married

g. buy a new bike

2. Fill in the blanks using the correct words from the box above.

1. I want to _____ around the world.
2. I'll _____ to my girlfriend in one year.
3. I will _____ soon. I need to lose some weight.

👥 Pair Work

Talk about future plans replacing the underlined words.

> A: What will you do <u>next year</u>?
> B: I will <u>learn the cello</u>.

80 CONNECTED 1

• Conversation • **Do You Have Any Plans for Next Year?**

1. Look at the picture and describe what is happening.

2. Listen to the conversation and fill in the blanks.

Everyone: 3… 2… 1… Happy New Year!
Jim: Do you have any plans for next year?
Becky: I want to _____ ___ _____ ___ _____. How about you?
Jim: I am going to _____ _____ _____, start a diet, and go to your _____ _____.
Becky: My pictures aren't that good.
Jim: Of course, they are. You have a great eye for photography.
Becky: If you say so… How about _____ with me this year? We can go anywhere.
Jim: Alright, let's go someplace warm.
Becky: Now you're talking! How about the Caribbean?
Jim: Oh, that's a great idea. I'm already excited for the trip.

Pair Work

Ask and answer about your plans for next year.

A: Do you have any plans for next year?
B: I'm going to travel around Europe.

• Grammar Point • Future with *Will*

Statements		Questions
Affirmative	Negative	
I **will** play games.	I **won't** play games.	**Will** you play games? What **will** you play?

1. Unscramble the words and complete the sentences using *will*.

1. When / she / have her concert / in Seoul / ?
   _____

2. They / fly / this afternoon / Japan / to / .
   _____

3. you / tomorrow / go to the movies / him / with / ?
   _____

4. treat you to lunch / I / not / next time / .
   _____

5. Jennifer and I / this evening / have Italian lessons / .
   _____

2. Look for grammatical errors. Rewrite the sentences correctly in future tense.

1. She goes to Paris this coming October.   _____
2. Benjamin watching a soccer game with Amy tonight. _____
3. I will be have an early dinner today.   _____
4. Will you buying this book for your mother?   _____
5. When will he washed the dishes?   _____

Pair Work

Practice this dialogue replacing the underlined words.

A: Will you <u>go to the party with me</u>?
B: Yes, I will. / No, I won't.

• Reading • Robots

1. What will the cars, houses, schools, and jobs be like in the future?

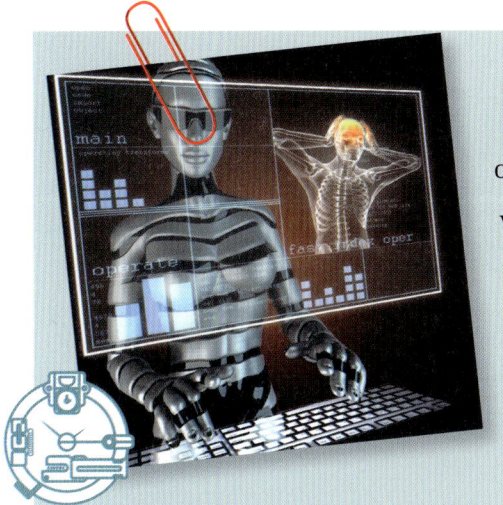

Do you think robots will be a part of our future lives? They are a part of our lives already and are becoming more common. We have robotic vacuum cleaners, car assembly robots, museum guidance robots, and surgical robots. Robots are used for medical purposes. Robots have changed the way diseases are treated. Medical researchers have developed nano-robots. They go inside the body of a cancer patient and help kill cancer cells. Robots have played a role in the military for some time. They have also helped police officers do some tasks, especially in dangerous situations. A number of U.S. schools are already adopting robots into the classroom, not as replacements for teachers, but as teaching assistants. Students can learn about biology, programming, crafts, public speaking, literacy, and air quality all at once. Robots can mix and connect across subjects freely. Robots will also be able to play music and make artwork for people to enjoy. A robot band called Compressorhead played at a Gibson booth at the Frankfurt Music Fair in 2013. Who knows? Maybe one day we can live longer via avatars.

[Reading Skill: Summarizing] Go to Page 110.

2. Read the passage. Write *T* for true or *F* for false for each statement.

1. Medical researchers have developed nano-robots that can kill cancer cells. _____
2. Robots can do all the tasks of police officers. _____
3. Robots have replaced teachers at many U.S. schools. _____

Group Work

Discuss these questions in a group.
- What other roles do you think Robots will play in the future?
- What do you think our lives will be like in the future?

Listen Up • It's My Plan!

1. Getting Ready Jacob is a heavy smoker, and his doctor advised him to quit smoking. Recently, he is also gaining weight, and he is worried about getting adult diseases. Check (√) the activities he should do to get healthy.

   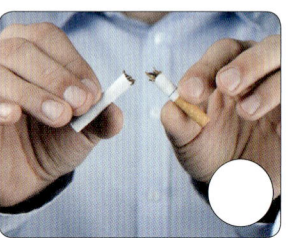

2. Easy Listening Listen to the dialogue and answer the questions.

1. What does the man suggest the woman do?
   a. take an exercise class   b. take a language class

2. When does the biking group meet?
   a. on Saturdays and Sundays   b. on Mondays and Tuesdays

3. What program will the woman sign up for?
   a. Cross Country Biking   b. none of the classes

3. Hard Rock Listen to the dialogue and answer the questions.

1. What is Jacob trying to do?
   a. quit smoking   b. smoke an e-cigarette

2. What did Val NOT suggest Jacob do to quit smoking?
   a. try e-cigarettes   b. take some medicine

4. Pronunciation Reduced Sound of *going to*
Listen and practice. Notice the reduced sound of *going to* in the sentences.

> I am **going to** go to the dentist. – I'm **gonna** go to the dentist.
> Are you **going to** practice the cello? – Are you **gonna** practice the cello?
> Where are they **going to** go? – Where are they **gonna** go?

• Speaking Build-up • What Are You Planning to Do?

1. Study the expressions to talk about future plans.

A: What are you going to do after finishing school?
B: I am going to visit my family back in India.
What about you?
A: I think I will try to find a part-time job.
B: Jobs are tough to find. Good luck.
A: Thanks, be safe on your trip. I'll see you when you come back.
B: Definitely!

A
- What are your plans?
- Any new goals for the future?
- Do you have any special plans?

B
- I'm planning to…
- I'm planning on *verb-ing*…
- Nothing too special.

2. Think of your plans for the near future using the topics given in the chart. Write down what you are planning to do.

Future plans	You	Your partner
diet	I'm planning to save 100 dollars a month.	He / She is planning to…
jobs		
travel		
saving money		
relationship		
school work		
buying something		
learning something		

 Pair Work

Practice this dialogue using the chart above. Write your partner's answers in the chart.

A: What are you planning to do next year?
B: I am going to quit smoking and drink less coffee.

Culture Awareness — New Year's Resolutions

Resolutions are usually made in January and mostly broken by March. It takes a strong will to keep a resolution and go for the entire year. Instead of stopping some bad habit, try starting something new. Make next year a chance to explore a new endeavor.

[Writing: New Year's Resolution] Go to Page 111.

Review Units 10~12

• Conversation • Watch out Next Time!

Listen to the conversation and fill in the blanks.

Becky: Josh, what happened?
Josh: Oh, I broke my arm last weekend.
Becky: How did it happen?
Josh: Well, last Friday, Mina and I went roller _____. And we fell down a lot.
Becky: I thought you _____ _____ very well.
Josh: _____ _____… To make matters worse, it even started to rain.
Becky: Did you slip in the rain?
Josh: Yes, we did. But that wasn't how it happened. We had a good time.
Becky: Okay, then what happened?
Josh: I was _____ _____ _____ after dinner. I hit my elbow on the sink. That's how I broke my arm.
Becky: Oh… You should be more careful in the future.
Josh: Don't worry. _____ _____ _____ be more careful.

👥 Pair Work

Think of one activity that you've done or learned. Then talk about it with your partner using the examples below.

- I started to learn to swim last year.
- Last year, I couldn't swim very well.
- I have practiced, so I can swim breaststroke this year.
- Next year, I will be able to swim butterfly.

Reading • Climate Change and Changing Life

Read the passage and choose the best answer to each question.

Last year, I was in London. I heard that climate change had affected the Tower of London. The Tower of London and Venice's famous canals are in danger of destruction because of flooding. Unbalanced weather puts world famous places at risk. Therefore, governments try to protect them.

Lake Superior is the world's largest freshwater lake. It is heating up and shrinking. Winter ice cover once reflected sunlight into space. Now, rising temperatures make it warm, so animals and plants can't live there. Boats and ships can't travel. Brazil gets 45% of its energy from nature. Climate change will affect its wind power, production of oil-producing crops, and power stations from rainfall. This will greatly impact the economy.

With warmer winter in the Arctic, we will have earlier springs and have longer and hotter summers. Large lakes are changing into ponds, and animals are moving farther south. Plants never seen in the area are growing. A 220-square-mile section of ice in Antarctica has fallen into the ocean. Changes in polar regions have changed sea levels and climate patterns across the world. Freshwater ice melting into saltwater oceans has changed water chemistry and harmed ocean animals. Over 300 million people in China have suffered from flash floods, landslides, drought, and water shortage due to climate change.

Climate change has changed our lives. What were they like before? What are they like now? Can you see the differences?

1. **What is happening to the Tower of London and Venice's famous canals?**
   a. Flooding puts them in danger of destruction.
   b. They are at risk because of wind.
   c. Freshwater harmed them.
   d. The sunlight has destroyed them.

2. **What is NOT true about Lake Superior?**
   a. It is heating and shrinking.
   b. It is causing temperatures to rise on the Earth.
   c. It is the world's largest freshwater lake.
   d. Animals and plants can no longer live there.

3. **Where does Brazil get 45% of its energy from?**
   a. from the jungle
   b. from oil
   c. from nature, such as rainfall and wind
   d. from sunlight

4. **What is NOT a thing China has suffered from?**
   a. flash floods
   b. drought
   c. earlier spring
   d. landslides

Unit 01

• Reading Skill •   Scanning for Details

> **Scanning**
> - a very high-speed reading technique
> - used when you are looking for a specific piece of information
> - to find the details quickly

Build up the Skill

1. Read the passages and answer the questions.

> Hey! My name is Mark and I'm a chef. I'm from Italy. I work in a restaurant and cook in the kitchen all afternoon and night. My specialty is pizza. I love cooking Italian food!

1. What is Mark's job?   He is a _____.
2. Where is Mark from?   He is _____.
3. Where does Mark work?   He works _____.
4. What is Mark's specialty?   His specialty is _____.

> Hello! I'm Rick. I'm a police officer in New York City. I'm from California. When I work, I drive around the city in my police car, help people, and catch criminals. At the end of the day, I go back to the police station and write a report.

5. What is the police officer's name?   His name is _____.
6. What does he do when he works?   He _____ around the city in his police car, _____, and _____ criminals.

> My grandmother is a great woman. She is from Korea. She has brown eyes and black hair. When she was 35, she moved to the United States. She speaks English very well now, but she couldn't before. She is very smart and kind. Her favorite food is kimchi.

7. Where is her grandmother from?   _____
8. What's her favorite food?   _____

Writing • About Yourself

1. Pre-writing Answer the following questions to prepare to write.

- Where are you from?
- What do you like to do in your free time?
- What is your favorite food?
- What is your dream for the future?

2. Writing the First Draft Write about yourself using the example below. Use the answers from the Pre-writing activity to organize your writing.

> **Example** I'd like to introduce a little bit about myself. My name is Jerry. I'm 23 years old. I'm from Turkey. I was born and raised in Istanbul. I came to Korea two years ago as an exchange student. I study International relations and Korean language here. I like riding a bike and cooking in my free time. I like to cook Turkish kebabs because it is my favorite. Sometimes I invite my friends and cook Kebabs for them. I hope to work for a Korean company after graduating from college.

Note If you are in Korea, and are asked "Where are you from?", say what city or province you are from. Only say "I am from Korea", if you are outside your home country.

3. Peer Review Exchange your writing with a partner. Then read your partner's writing and look for mistakes or errors. Make corrections on them and return the writing to your partner.

4. Rewriting Look at the corrections that your partner made and revise your writing based on the corrections. Try to rewrite the parts you'd like to change in order to improve your writing.

Unit 02

• Reading Skill • Skimming

Skimming
- a high-speed reading technique
- to get the general idea of a passage, not specific details(scanning)

Build up the Skill

1. Read the passages and answer the questions.

Hello there! I'm Sarah and I am a third-grade teacher from Michigan. Teaching keeps me very busy, but I truly love what I do for a living. I teach for 6 hours a day. My day begins at 8:00 a.m. and finishes at 2:00 p.m. I teach Monday through Friday, but on weekends and after school, I coach softball. It's a busy life, but I like it that way.

1. What is Sarah's job? Her job is a _____.

"Hippo" is a nickname of the animal hippopotamus, which means river horse. The hippopotamus was once found across Africa. Today, however, Africans hunt many hippos. Thus, the animal moved to Eastern and Central Africa.
One of the African folk tales tells how God created the hippos. God told the hippos to cut grass for the other animals. Africa was very hot and dry. So the Hippos wanted to stay in the water during the day and cut the grass at night because the weather was cool at night times. God said it was okay, but he worried about the hippo eating fish in the river. So he made them only to eat plants.

2. What is the main idea of this story?

   a. A folk tale about hippos
   b. Hippo's favorite food
   c. Hippos' life and death
   d. How to protect hippos

Thomas Edison is one of the greatest people in history. He invented many useful things. People called him a wizard because of his many important inventions. His major inventions are the phonograph (record player), the light bulb, and the motion-picture projector. He also created the first power station in the United States in 1882.
Thomas Edison was born in 1847 in Ohio. He lost his hearing when he was very young. He did poorly in school because he could not hear his teacher. But he was creative and curious.

So his mother educated him at home. Thomas loved to read and experiment with many things. When he was 12 years old, he began to sell newspapers on trains. Then he worked as a telegraph operator. He was good at sending and taking messages in Morse code. At the age of 22, he quit his job and became a full-time inventor.

3. What is this story mainly about?

   a. How Edison invented the light bulb
   b. Edison's research lab
   c. How Edison lost his hearing
   d. Edison's life and inventions

• Writing • Your Family Members' Jobs

1. Pre-writing Answer the following questions to prepare to write.

- What is your job?
- What do your parents do?
- What do your siblings do for a living?

2. Writing the First Draft Write about your family members' jobs. Use the answers from the Pre-writing activity to organize your writing.

 I am the black sheep* in my family. My mother and father are both nurses. Both of my aunts and one of my uncles are also nurses. Even my brother is a nurse. When we get together, they always talk about medicine. I can usually follow along, but it makes my head hurt. The only other person who is not a nurse is my sister-in-law, and we are both teachers.
*black sheep – this usually refers to someone that is different from other members of their family or follows a nontraditional path in life.

Note Asking people about their family's professions can be a sensitive subject. So, only give as much information as you feel comfortable with. If your father is the CEO of Hyundai, you might say he is a manager in a car company. You can be correct, without being specific.

3. Peer Review Exchange your writing with a partner. Then read your partner's writing and look for mistakes or errors. Make corrections on them and return the writing to your partner.

4. Rewriting Look at the corrections that your partner made and revise your writing based on the corrections. Try to rewrite the parts you'd like to change in order to improve your writing.

Unit 03

• Reading Skill • Identifying the Topic and Main Idea

> **A paragraph** usually includes: topic, main idea (or a topic sentence), and supporting details.
> **Topic** is the general subject of a written passage.
> **Identifying a topic** can help you find the author's main idea.
> **Topic sentence** is the broadest and most focused statement in a paragraph.

Build up the Skill

1. Write the topic of the following sentences.

- Most scientists agree that temperatures now are warmer than 20 years ago.
- It's hard to know the exact consequences of climate change.
- The Earth has been getting warmer over the last several thousand years, not just the last 50 years.

Topic: _____

2. Write the topic sentence of each paragraph.

Colors appear to affect how we feel. There is evidence that supports the idea that certain colors have an effect on our bodies. When you look at the color red your heart may tend to beat more, but look at blue and it will beat less. Our eyes also react differently to the same colors; red tends to make us blink more often, while blue allows us to do it less often. Our feelings and the colors that are associated with them appear to be consistent. Another example of how colors affect us was shown in a school. When the color of the walls was changed to blue from orange and white, students felt less pressure and their overall academic performance improved.

1. **Topic Sentence:** _____

Animals sleep in a number of ways. How much do you sleep every day? Probably about 8 hours per day. However, not all animals sleep for the same amount of time. Some animals sleep during the day while others sleep at night. The length of time that they sleep can also be affected by the time of year. There are animals that can sleep for weeks or even months at a time as they often hibernate during winter.

*hibernate: to sleep through the winter

2. Topic Sentence: _____

• Writing • Know Your Surroundings

1. Pre-writing Look around your classroom for one minute. Try to remember where things are. Then answer the following questions.

- Where is the teacher's desk?
- Where is the projector?
- What's next to the door?
- What's under the windows?

2. Writing the First Draft Write the descriptions of your classroom based on your memory. Use the answers from the Pre-writing activity to organize your writing.

> **Example** My classroom is a very large room. The teacher has a podium in front of the room. Next to the podium, there is a computer work station. On the front wall, behind the teacher's podium, there is a chalkboard and screen. Three radiators are under the windows. There are two doors to get into the classroom, one in the front of the room and the other in the back.

3. Peer Review Exchange your writing with a partner. Then read your partner's writing and look for mistakes or errors. Make corrections on them and return the writing to your partner.

4. Rewriting Look at the corrections that your partner made and revise your writing based on the corrections. Try to rewrite the parts you'd like to change in order to improve your writing.

Unit 04

• Reading Skill • Finding Supporting Details

> **Supporting details** are reasons, examples, facts, steps, or other kinds of evidence that back up and explain a main idea.

Build up the Skill

1. Read the passage and answer the questions.

> A healthy life starts off by eating a healthy diet. First, get a good start to your day by eating breakfast every day. This will make you start your day on the right path. Be sure to eat a balanced meal for lunch and dinner. If you feel hungry between meals, have a healthy snack and avoid junk food. You should wait at least four hours between each meal or snack. Eating three good meals a day will help you stay healthy and feel better.

1. Which of these are NOT supporting details in the paragraph?
   a. Get a good start to your day by eating breakfast every day.
   b. Be sure to eat a balanced meal for lunch and dinner.
   c. If you feel hungry between meals, have a healthy snack and avoid junk food.
   d. Eating three good snacks a day will help you stay healthy and help you feel better.

2. The purpose of the supporting details in this paragraph is to give _____.
   a. the reasons why you have to eat healthy food throughout the day
   b. the examples of good meals and snacks that can be eaten throughout the day
   c. the suggestions for making healthier food choices
   d. the importance of balanced meals

2. Choose three sentences that logically support the main idea.

1. **Main Idea: Drinking coffee can be bad for people.** _____, _____, _____
   a. Some people don't like the taste of decaffeinated coffee.
   b. Coffee in the evening makes people unable to sleep at night.
   c. When it comes to addictions, coffee is less dangerous than tobacco.
   d. Too much coffee can make your hands shake.
   e. Drinking too much coffee makes your heart beat faster.
   f. Most coffees are under five dollars per kilogram.

2. Main Idea: Some people have very poor telephone manners. _____, _____, _____

   a. They never introduce themselves, but just start talking.
   b. They often make their calls on cell phones.
   c. They have an unlisted telephone number.
   d. They speak with people around them while they're talking on the phone.
   e. Some people don't like to talk on the phone.
   f. They often call around lunch or dinner time.

• Writing • An Item that You Want to Sell or Get Rid of

1. Pre-writing Answer the following questions to prepare to write.

> - Is there an item you want to sell or get rid of?
> - How much money do you want for the item?
> - What are the features or faults with the item?

2. Writing the First Draft Imagine that you're selling an item online. Write an advertisement to sell the items based on your answers from the Pre-writing activity.

> **Example** Nintendo Wii for sale $150 OBO*.
> I am selling a Nintendo Wii with two controllers and ten games. The game system is two years old and has rarely been used. It is in a really good condition and ready for someone to take it home immediately. Please send me a message at stuffforsale@goodmail.com or call me at 012-345-6789.
> *OBO stands for the term Or Best Offer which means the price can be a little discounted than presented.

> **Note** When you sell an item online, it is often best to post the item on a social media website to advertise it. Pictures help and get people interested in the item. If you post on a social media site, you may be asked to PM (Private Message) a person with more information. But remember not to give your personal information to them because it can be risky.

3. Peer Review Exchange your writing with a partner. Then read your partner's writing and look for mistakes or errors. Make corrections on them and return the writing to your partner.

4. Rewriting Look at the corrections that your partner made and revise your writing based on the corrections. Try to rewrite the parts you'd like to change in order to improve your writing.

Unit 05

• Reading Skill • Facts and Opinions

Facts tell real information that can be proven true.
Opinions are what someone thinks or feels.

Build up the Skill

1. Write *F* for fact or *O* for opinion for each sentence.

1. Mr. Jones has two sons and one daughter. _____
2. That picture is by Rembrandt. _____
3. Her house is really beautiful. _____
4. My friend has five brothers. _____
5. That boy is the nicest person in the school. _____
6. Frank Baum wrote "The Wizard of Oz". _____
7. The Bulls are better than the Knicks. _____
8. Nine plus one equals ten. _____
9. I really like the weather there because it is always warm. _____
10. They never laugh at my bad Spanish. _____
11. Mexico City has many interesting places to visit. _____
12. It has lots of amazing old buildings and some interesting museums. _____

2. Read the passage. Write one fact and one opinion sentence from the passage.

> Julian Moore is an American–British actress and children's author. As Alice Howland, she played a college professor suffering from early-onset Alzheimer. She was nominated for Academy Award five times, and she became the winner in 2015. She is very diligent and has a beautiful smile. I think her screenplay is very subtle and sensitive.

1. Fact

2. Opinion

Writing • Directions to the House Party

1. Pre-writing Answer the following questions to prepare to write.

- What are the major landmarks around your home?
- What are the buses or subways that come close to your home?
- What does your house look like?
- What is your home address? How can I get there?

2. Writing the First Draft Pretend that you're having a housewarming party. Write an invitation card to your classmates and give them directions to your place.

> **Example** I am having a house party on Saturday. The party will start at 7:00 p.m. and should finish around midnight. If you would like to come, please take the subway red line to the last stop. It's called Lockheed Station. Go out of exit 7 and walk straight for 200 meters. At the bread store, turn right and go another 50 meters. Look for the Pizzeria and enter the building on the right side. Take the elevator to the 7th floor. My apartment is 702, almost at the end of the hallway. See you there.

3. Peer Review Exchange your writing with a partner. Then read your partner's writing and look for mistakes or errors. Make corrections on them and return the writing to your partner.

4. Rewriting Look at the corrections that your partner made and revise your writing based on the corrections. Try to rewrite the parts you'd like to change in order to improve your writing.

Unit 06

• Reading Skill • Sequencing

> **Sequencing** or time order refers to putting events or actions in order. The order of events are often used with connecting words such as *first, next, then, lastly, and finally* at the end. These words help the readers to understand how things are linked to one another in time order in a passage.

Build up the Skill

1. Read the passage and complete the sentences in chronological order.

> Alphonse has a great job working in a bakery. The first thing he does every day is to wake up and go to work. His day begins before the sun rises. He walks quickly to work because the streets are still empty. Next, Alphonse works to help the baker make rolls and pastries. Then they put the large metal trays in the oven and wait for the bread to cook. The delicious smells of baking rolls and bread fill the shop and make them both very hungry. While the bread bakes, they eat breakfast together. Alphonse is learning to make delicious pastries from the very kind baker.

1. The first thing he does every day is _____ to work.
2. He _____ because the streets are still empty.
3. Next, Alphonse works to _____ the baker _____.
4. _____ fill the shop.
5. Then they _____ together.

2. Read the passage and answer the following questions.

> One late night I was walking home from visiting my grandfather. It was only a few minutes until nine. I needed to hurry so I wouldn't be late. When I got to the corner of Maple Avenue, I heard a strange sound. It sounded like someone crying. I looked around and found a small gray kitten. It looked about five weeks old; it had its eyes open and could walk around. Still, it was pretty small. I stopped and tried to pet the kitten. It ran away from me. I really wanted to take it home with me, but I heard my mom's voice in my head. I could hear her telling me we can't take care of any more cats. We already had three. True, Tiger was old and we had to take him to the vet last week. We couldn't afford another cat. I wasn't sure what to do, so I took a ham sandwich out of my bag. The kitten was too shy or scared to come and eat it. I didn't want to be late, so I put the sandwich down on the sidewalk. I just left the cat behind and went home. Maybe the cat ate it. That night I couldn't sleep. I thought about the kitten and hoped it was okay. I felt bad and thought that there was more I should do to help it. Next morning, I woke up and went out to look for the kitten near the corner. I didn't see it anywhere. I hoped that someone found it and took it home.

1. **Why didn't the writer take the kitten home?**
   a. He was worried about its health.
   b. He knew he couldn't afford to keep it.
   c. He felt sorry for his mom.
   d. He wasn't sure whether he liked it.

2. **What happened after the writer took the sandwich out of the bag?**
   a. The kitten came up to the writer.
   b. He thought about what his mom would say.
   c. He asked his mom if he could keep it.
   d. He put the sandwich on the sidewalk.

3. **What did he do after he woke up?**
   a. He felt bad.
   b. He went to look for the kitten.
   c. He came back and ate the meat.
   d. He helped the cat.

• Writing • My Daily Routine

1. Pre-writing Answer the following questions to prepare to write.

- When do you usually wake up and eat breakfast?
- When do you get to school or work?
- What do you do after dinner?
- What do you usually do before you go to bed?

2. Writing the First Draft Write about your daily routine using the example below. Use the answers from the Pre-writing activity to organize your writing.

> **Example** My day is fairly routine. I wake up every morning at 7:15. Usually, my birds start chirping and want their breakfast at that time. I get up and wash my face. After getting dressed, my fiancée and I sit and talk over a cup of coffee. At 8:30, I walk to work. I usually start work at 9:00. I have lunch with my coworkers around 1:00. At 6:30 I meet my fiancée at the bus stop. We walk home and shop in the local stores. We usually watch TV in the evening. At 10:00, I usually take a shower, or sometimes I take a bath. At 11:00, I go to bed and read a book until I feel sleepy.

> **Note** It is not uncommon for unmarried people to live together in Western countries. Many couples that are engaged will live together before they get married.

3. Peer Review Exchange your writing with a partner. Then read your partner's writing and look for mistakes or errors. Make corrections on them and return the writing to your partner.

4. Rewriting Look at the corrections that your partner made and revise your writing based on the corrections. Try to rewrite the parts you'd like to change in order to improve your writing.

Unit 07

• Reading Skill • Scanning for Details

Scanning is to look for a certain fact or important information in a passage rather than to read the whole passage. You scan information by picking out certain keywords.

Build up the Skill

1. If the instruction is mentioned in the passage, check (√) **Yes**, if not, check **No**.

> Natural gas has an artificial smell added to it to let us know if there is a leak. If you smell that strange smell, you should immediately extinguish any fires or open flames. Do not turn on any electrical devices or touch any switches. Don't even use your telephone or cellular phone. Exit the building and call the gas company from a neighbor's phone. If you are unable to contact your gas supplier, call the Fire Department.

Instructions	Yes	No
Turn on the stove.		
Touch the electrical switch.		
Extinguish any open flame.		
Call your gas supplier.		
Do not use phones in the building.		
Do not touch liquids.		
Open windows.		
Call the Police Department.		

2. Look at the table of *Mercury Levels in Fish* and answer the questions.

1. Which fish are low in mercury?
   a. Atlantic mackerel   b. Sea trout
   c. Shark   d. Bluefish

2. If you're trying to eat fish that is lower in mercury, which one of these is the best choice?
   a. Striped bass   b. Sea trout
   c. Sardine   d. Tuna (canned albacore)

Mercury* Levels in Fish	
Atlantic mackerel	Low
Bluefish	High
Flounder	Low
Grouper	High
Halibut	Medium
Sardine	Low
Sea trout	Medium
Shark	High
Skate	Medium
Striped bass	Medium
Tuna (Canned albacore)	High
Tuna (canned light)	Low/Medium

* Mercury: silver-colored liquid metal that is used especially in thermometers and barometers. If levels are high in food, we should avoid eating it.

3. Which of these four fish is the highest in mercury?

   a. Skate   b. Halibut   c. Striped bass   d. Bluefish

4. Which of the following fish has the lowest amount of mercury in it?

   a. Flounder   b. Shark   c. Sea trout   d. Grouper

5. Write *T* for true or *F* for false for the statement.

   The chart does not have a listing for shrimp. _____

• Writing • What Makes You Like Someone?

1. Pre-writing Answer the following questions to prepare to write.

- Is there anyone you like?
- What does he/she look like? Is he/she short or tall?
- What kind of personality does he/she have?
- Does what he/she look like matters to you a lot?

2. Writing the First Draft Write about the reasons why you like someone referring to the example below. Use the answers from the Pre-writing activity to organize your writing.

> **Example** While some people think that a Hollywood celebrity should look tall, thin and beautiful, I think it is the person's confidence that really makes them attractive. Camryn Manheim is a very large and rather tall woman. She has been acting for many years. She has self-confidence and has worked with deaf people. She is fluent in sign language and has used her skills to help deaf mothers during labor. The most beautiful thing to put on is not your clothes, but your smile.

3. Peer Review Exchange your writing with a partner. Then read your partner's writing and look for mistakes or errors. Make corrections on them and return the writing to your partner.

4. Rewriting Look at the corrections that your partner made and revise your writing based on the corrections. Try to rewrite the parts you'd like to change in order to improve your writing.

Unit 08

• Reading Skill • Skimming

Skimming
- used to quickly identify the main ideas of a text
- to read at a speed three to four times faster than normal reading

Build up the Skill

Read the passages and answer the questions.

> Now Janet is in her house. She is sitting on a wooden chair. She is holding a coat. She is fixing it. James is Janet's husband. He is sitting in front of her. He is fixing clothes too. Elizabeth is sitting next to James. She is Janet's sister. Right now she is helping Janet and James. They are working together. They are fixing clothes.

1. Who is James? _____
2. Where is James? _____
3. What is James doing? _____
4. Who is Elizabeth? _____
5. What is Elizabeth doing? _____

> Right now, it is Monday morning. Mike and Tina are at home. They are sitting at a table. They are eating breakfast. At this moment, Tina is drinking coffee. She is eating a pastry. She is sitting across the table from Mike. She is talking to Mike. Mike is Tina's husband. He is also drinking coffee. Mike is listening to Tina. After breakfast, Mike and Tina are leaving for work. They work in the city. They are riding the bus to work.

6. What is Tina eating? _____
7. Where is Tina sitting? _____
8. What is Mike drinking? _____
9. What is Mike doing? _____
10. Where are they going after breakfast? _____

Today, Abby is visiting her grandparents. At this moment, she is sitting on her grandfather's knee. She is listening to a story. She is smiling. She loves her grandfather's stories. Jacob is Abby's grandfather. He loves his granddaughter. Right now, he is telling her a story. He is holding her on his knee. He is holding her hands. They are sitting in the living room.

11. Where is Abby visiting? _____
12. What is Abby doing? _____
13. What is Jacob doing? _____
14. What is the story mainly about?

    a. Abby and her grandfather   b. Abby's grandparents
    c. Abby's grandfather and his story   d. books and cookies

• Writing • What Is Your Favorite Free Time Activity?

1. Pre-writing Answer the following questions to prepare to write.

- What do you like to do in your free time?
- Do you like to play video games / board games?
- Do you collect anything?
- How often do you read the newspaper / books / blogs / emails?

2. Writing the First Draft Write about your free time activities using the example below. Use the answers from the Pre-writing activity to organize your writing.

> **Example** I am a workaholic. That means that I usually work 13 to 15 hours a day. It is a crazy life and full of stress. On those few free days I have, I love to build with Lego bricks. I create amazing things. Sometimes I follow the instructions, but other times I create my own idea. When I am building, I usually listen to audio books. I don't have time to read books, so I do love to be read instead. Audio books allow me to work and listen at the same time.

3. Peer Review Exchange your writing with a partner. Then read your partner's writing and look for mistakes or errors. Make corrections on them and return the writing to your partner.

4. Rewriting Look at the corrections that your partner made and revise your writing based on the corrections. Try to rewrite the parts you'd like to change in order to improve your writing.

Unit 09

• Reading Skill • Identifying the Topic and Main Idea

> **Topic** is what the paragraph is about.
> **Main Idea** = Topic + Author's message or point
> **Main Idea** is the overall message or argument being made by the author about the topic of the paragraph.

Build up the Skill

Read the passages and answer the questions.

> One of the most destructive pests in the world is the fire ant. They got this nickname because of the painful burning sensation that comes after being stung by one. Fire ants use a wasp-like stinger* to inject its poisonous venom. The venom causes a painful burning sensation and small itchy red spots. These ants will usually attack anything or anyone that gets too close to their nests. Not only do they cause pain when they sting, but they also have a nasty habit of destroying plants. They particularly like soybeans, corns, eggplants, okras, strawberries, and potatoes. These ants are truly little pests with a fiery sting.
>
> *wasp-like stinger: a bee's stinger that is used as a defensive weapon against someone or something

1. What is the topic of the passage?

   a. insects b. farming crops c. fire ants d. pet ants

2. What does the author want you to know from the passage?

   a. Fire ants have painful bites. b. Fire ants only eat plants.
   c. Fire ants move in swarms. d. Fire ants are painful pests.

3. Which sentence contains the main idea? Find the sentence and write it.

   _____

> After a long hard day of work as a seamstress (sewing clothes) a woman got on a bus and sat down. She was asked to move to the back of the bus because of the color of her skin. Her name was Rosa Parks, an African-American woman in the 1960s. She lived in Montgomery, Alabama where it had the law for people of color to sit in the back of the bus. She refused to give up her seat and move to the back of the bus. All because she said "NO" she went to jail. This act of defiance received national attention. Many people believe that her refusal to give up her seat and move to the back of the bus signaled the beginning of the civil rights movement. Rosa Parks was a truly brave woman and showed us that one person's bravery can change the world.

4. What is the topic of the passage?
   a. Rosa Parks	b. Civil Rights	c. Buses	d. The 1970s

5. What does the author want you to know from the passage?
   a. All people of color are African American.
   b. Special buses are needed.
   c. Rosa Parks was a crazy stubborn woman.
   d. Brave people can make a difference.

6. Which sentence contains the main idea? Find the sentence and write it.

___

• Writing • Which One Do You Like More?

1. Pre-writing Answer the following questions to prepare to write.

- What do you like shopping for the most?
- Why do you like shopping for it (them)?
- Is a brand-name product better than a generic product?
- Which is more important, price or value?

2. Writing the First Draft Write about what you like shopping for the most. Use the answers from the Pre-writing activity to organize your writing.

> **Example** I don't like going shopping. I am always debating which shirt is prettier, or if I should buy the most expensive brand or the cheapest. For me, shopping for clothes is the most boring activity, but I like shopping for electronic items the most. Comparing and testing the new computers is a lot of fun. It is great to see which computers are faster and how much bigger the computers' memories are getting.

3. Peer Review Exchange your writing with a partner. Then read your partner's writing and look for mistakes or errors. Make corrections on them and return the writing to your partner.

4. Rewriting Look at the corrections that your partner made and revise your writing based on the corrections. Try to rewrite the parts you'd like to change in order to improve your writing.

Unit 10

• Reading Skill • Finding Supporting Details

Supporting Details = Information that supports the main idea or specifically talks about it

Build up the Skill

Read the passages and answer the questions.

> The shopping plazas, housing areas and the middle of the highways in Florida are decorated with many beautiful plants. These amazing plants help make Florida have a tropical feel. The royal palm is a very tall plant that can grow to nearly ninety feet tall. They tower over many hotels and shopping centers. Closer to the ground, you will find the Hibiscus plant everywhere. It has beautiful red, pink, and orange flowers and looks good almost everywhere. You may find them near some of Florida's hotels, homes, and some businesses. The last plant you may want to encounter is called saw palmetto. This plant really earns its name and works as a great way to create a natural barrier between houses or even roads. Florida has many beautiful places, but the plants make it truly tropical.

1. What is the main idea? _____

2. Which area in Florida is NOT decorated with tropical plants?
   a. shopping centers
   b. middle of highway
   c. inside buildings
   d. houses

3. What is one of the most beautiful and towering tall tree? _____

4. What plant looks good anywhere? _____

5. Where does the saw palmetto work well? _____

> The best way to see a movie is at a drive-in theater. These outdoor theaters had their beginnings in 1933 in Riverton, New Jersey. Richard Hollingshead, Jr., set up a movie screen in front of his garage. Later that year, he opened a real drive-in theater in the town of Camden. This theater had room for 400 cars. What a clever idea!

6. What is the topic? _____

7. When did the drive-in theater begin? _____

8. Who made the first drive-in theater? _____

9. Where did the first real drive-in theater open first? _____

10. How much room did the real drive-in theater have? _____

• Writing • What a Weekend!

1. Pre-writing Answer the following questions to prepare to write.

> - Did you do anything special last weekend? What did you do?
> - Did any special occasions or events happen last week?
> - Did you have any adventures or a narrow escape?

2. Writing the First Draft Write about what you did or what happened to you last weekend. Use the answers from the Pre-writing activity to organize your writing.

> **Example** You will never believe what happened to me last weekend. I was coming home from work and a bus nearly hit me. It jumped the curb and came within inches of hitting me. And then it got worse. I got to my house and found the front door opened. Someone had broken into my house and stolen everything. The only good thing is I am insured.

3. Peer Review Exchange your writing with a partner. Then read your partner's writing and look for mistakes or errors. Make corrections on them and return the writing to your partner.

4. Rewriting Look at the corrections that your partner made and revise your writing based on the corrections. Try to rewrite the parts you'd like to change in order to improve your writing.

Unit 11

• Reading Skill • Facts and Opinions

> **Facts** are something that can be proved to be true.
> **Opinions** are a personal feeling or belief about something.

Build up the Skill

1. Read the statement. Write *F* for fact or *O* for opinion for each statement.

1. A giant tortoise can live for 150 years or more. _____
2. A polar bear is the most fun animal to watch. _____
3. Usually bald eagles lay one to two eggs at a time. _____
4. The bats in the cave are very scary. _____
5. Cheetahs can run faster than lions. _____

2. Read the passage. Write *F* for fact or *O* for opinion for each statement.

> One of my biggest heroes was Jackie Robinson. His courage and determination showed us that it doesn't matter what color your skin is and it only matters how good you are at what you do. Jackie was the first black man to play professional baseball in the United States.
> Robinson was born into a poor family in Georgia in 1919. His mother worked as a maid to make money to raise Jackie and his four brothers and sisters. His father had left them while Jackie was still a baby. The Robinsons moved to California while Jackie was a child. People used to admire how good Jackie was at sports. As a well-rounded athlete, he played not only baseball but also football and basketball in high school. Jackie was always a fast runner and started playing on a baseball team for black players when he was 25.
> When the owner of the Brooklyn Dodgers saw Jackie play, he asked him to play in the professional league. In the beginning, his fellow teammates didn't like Jackie. They ignored him and never spoke to him just because he was black. But, he never gave up and worked harder and harder. By the end of his first year, he had been voted the Most Valuable Player and the Rookie of the Year. It just goes to show you that through determination you can do anything. That is why I think he is the greatest baseball player ever and he is my hero.

1. He was the first Black man to play on a major league baseball team. _____
2. At the end of his first season, he was voted the Most Valuable Player and Rookie of the Year. _____
3. In high school he played football, basketball, and baseball. _____
4. Jackie Robinson is a hero. _____
5. In 1919, Jackie was born in Georgia. _____
6. Jackie Robinson is the greatest baseball ever. _____
7. When he was growing up, people admired Jackie. _____

• Writing • What's Your Favorite Sport?

1. Pre-writing Answer the following questions to prepare to write.

- What kind of sports or activities do you like?
- Do you like team or individual activities?
- Do you prefer watching a game on television or sitting in the stands?
- Do you think games with a lot of rules are more fun than simple games?

2. Writing the First Draft Write about a sport or activity you like to do. Use the answers from the Pre-writing activity to organize your writing.

> **Example** Sports can be a lot of fun. There is a perfect sport out there for each of us. I personally love to go and spend a few hours chasing a little white ball around a green field. Okay, it is actually golf. I do love the feeling when I am out there. The fresh air and exercise do me so much good.

3. Peer Review Exchange your writing with a partner. Then read your partner's writing and look for mistakes or errors. Make corrections on them and return the writing to your partner.

4. Rewriting Look at the corrections that your partner made and revise your writing based on the corrections. Try to rewrite the parts you'd like to change in order to improve your writing.

Unit 12

• Reading Skill • Summarizing

Summarizing
- to reduce a large selection of text to the main points for more concise understanding
- to determine essential ideas
- to consolidate important details that support essential ideas
- to focus on keywords and phrases
- to cross out redundant, highly detailed, or unimportant information

Build up the Skill

Read the passages and answer the questions.

In North America, the largest member of the cat family is the mountain lion, also known as a cougar. They are powerful and beautiful creatures, but they are also wild animals and must be respected. When a mountain lion is fully grown it can weigh between 90 pounds and as much as 200 pounds or more. Most of these big cats weigh about 110 pounds and can be around six feet long from nose to the tip of its tail. Like all wild cats, they are carnivorous. That means that they eat meat. Mountain lions kill many small animals like skunks and rabbits. But, they will hunt and kill bigger animals such as deer and elk. Ranchers don't like mountain lions because they occasionally kill cattle, sheep, horses, and even dogs. They like to be left alone and are often very secretive. They live in rocky areas with lots of brushes which make them difficult to find. They are also fiercely territorial, which means that they usually hunt and live in the same area or territory. These territories can cover many square miles. Although the cougar is a beautiful animal, it is very wild. That means that it is fierce and often dangerous. We must respect these powerful animals when we enter their territory, or end up being hunted.

1. What is the main idea? _____

2. Check (√) the essential ideas.

   _____ a. The mountain lions are the largest member of the cat family living in North America.

   _____ b. Mountain lions are carnivorous.

   _____ c. Most of the mountain lions weigh about 120 pounds.

   _____ d. Because mountain lions are very secretive, they are hard to find.

   _____ e. The cougars are very territorial.

   _____ f. The cougars are beautiful animals, but they are very strong and can be very fierce and dangerous.

   _____ g. The cougars eat only larger animals such as deer, elk and even eat cattle, and horses.

Kayla and Kiki are dolphins living at the local sea park and aquarium. They are the stars of a special kind of show. Audiences come from all around to watch them perform. Both of them know many special tricks like jumping through hoops, walking across the water and leaping up high to catch fish. To walk across the water they use their powerful tails.

Each of them weighs about 400 pounds and is 12 feet long. Their trainer has helped them learn many amazing tricks. They learned some tricks on their own, like being able to hold their breath for about 15 minutes. People really enjoy learning about these amazing animals and going to see Kayla and Kiki perform.

3. Who is this story about? _____
4. How did they learn their amazing tricks? _____

• Writing • New Year's Resolution

1. Pre-writing Answer the following questions to prepare to write.

> Pretend you're making a New Year's resolution.
> - What is your New Year's resolution?
> - What do you want to achieve this year?
> - What will you do to keep your New Year's resolution?

2. Writing the First Draft Write about your New Year's resolutions referring to the following example. Use the answers from the Pre-writing activity to organize your writing.

> **Example** I need to lose 22 pounds by June. I want to go to the beach next summer and wear a sexy bikini. To do so, I will have to go to the gym four days a week and watch what I eat. I can't have any more snacks or soda. I also want to improve my English. I need to spend an hour a day practicing. Maybe I should watch TV dramas or even online videos in English.

3. Peer Review Exchange your writing with a partner. Then read your partner's writing and look for mistakes or errors. Make corrections on them and return the writing to your partner.

4. Rewriting Look at the corrections that your partner made and revise your writing based on the corrections. Try to rewrite the parts you'd like to change in order to improve your writing.

Script

Unit 01 | Script

Conversation

James: Hi Angela. This is my friend, David. David, this is Angela.
David: Hi. I'm glad to meet you.
Angela: Nice to meet you. Where are you from?
David: I'm from Germany. And you?
Angela: I'm from Italy.
David: Do you speak German?
Angela: Only a little, but I understand when someone speaks to me in German.
David: That's still very nice.

Listen Up

2. Easy Listening

Kevin: Hello, this is Kevin.
Chris: Hey, Kevin.
Kevin: Hi, Chris. What's up?
Chris: Do you know Alice and John's numbers?
Kevin: Yes, I do. Alice's mobile number is 016-3216-1274, and John's home number is 711-3469.
Chris: Thanks, Kevin.

3. Hard Rock

WTMI Radio is proud to present people of note in the 21st century. Our first person is Barack Obama. He was born in 1961 in Hawaii. His father was born in Kenya and his mother was an American Citizen. He attended Harvard Law School and became a lawyer and professor. In 2008 he became the first African-American President of the United States.

Unit 02 | Script

Conversation

Bob: Hello, Mary. Long time no see.
Mary: Oh, hi, Bob! It is good to see you. How are you?
Bob: Just fine, I remember you work at Florence Hospital as a nurse. Do you still work there?
Mary: No, I moved to Charity Hospital. It's downtown. Where do you work now?
Bob: Oh, I have my own company as a computer programmer.
Mary: Really? Where is your office?
Bob: I usually work at home, but I can work anywhere.

Listen Up

2. Easy Listening

A: Do you have a part-time job?
B: Actually, I have three.
A: Wow! What are they?
B: On Tuesdays and Thursdays, I work at the school cafeteria as a busboy.
A: And, your second job?
B: On Mondays, Wednesdays, and Fridays I am a barista at a café.
A: So, when do you do your last job?
B: Oh, right! I babysit my little brother and sister on Friday and Saturday nights.

3. Hard Rock

A: Hello Darrell, will you tell me about your career?
B: Sure. I did odd jobs, when I was a kid. At 18, I became a soldier in the air force.
A: What did you do next?
B: I went to nursing school and became a nurse.
A: Did you do any other work at the hospital?
B: I worked as a purchasing manager for the hospital for many years. Then I took some time off. Now I'm back to work full time as a nurse. It's great.
A: All right. Thank you!

Unit 03 | Script

Conversation

Peter: What's wrong, Wendy?
Wendy: I can't find my wallet.
Peter: Really? When did you have it last?
Wendy: That's the problem. I don't remember.
Peter: Is it in your bag?
Wendy: No, that's the first place I looked. And I checked here and there, but I can't find it.
Peter: Well, what did you do yesterday?
Wendy: I was shopping online, and I needed my credit card…
Peter: Is that it? Next to the computer?
Wendy: That's it! Thank you.

Listen Up

1. Getting Ready

a. The lamp is on the night table.
b. The dress is on the bed.
c. The earrings are under the table.
d. The dishes are in the dishwasher.
e. The ring is on top of the television.

2. Easy Listening

A: You look serious. What's wrong?
B: I have looked everywhere and cannot find my glasses.
A: Really? I know where they are!
B: Please tell me.
A: Let's play a game to help you find them.
B: Ugghhh… Alright, tell me.
A: If it's not under something, it is…
B: On top of it. But I don't see them.
A: There are two places that we cannot see without the aid of a mirror.
B: Sure, you can't see your back or… or…UGGHH.
A: Or, on top of your head.

3. Hard Rock

Man: Are you ready to go shopping for Christmas presents?
Woman: Yes, but it's going to take us all day.
Man: Why do you say that?
Woman: Well, we need to buy a CD for Johnny and a watch for Mike.
Man: And we need to buy some books and pens for June.
Woman: Don't forget we also need a bike for little Mary.
Man: You're right. This will take us all day.
Woman: Well, we could go shopping in one place…
Man: Please don't say we are going to the mall.
Woman: I know it's busy, but we can buy everything in one place.

Review Units 01~03

Conversation

Security: Welcome to the United States, may I see your passport?
Peter: Sure here you are.
Security: It says you are from Korea. Are you here on business or pleasure?
Peter: Business, unfortunately.
Security: What kind of business are you in?
Peter: I am in sales for new cars. I work for a Korean car company.
Security: Okay. May I see your return ticket, please?
Peter: Sure… Wait… I just had it. It's not in my pocket. Where did I leave it?
Security: Sir?
Peter: Yes?
Security: Sir, it's in your other hand with your jacket.
Peter: Oh, thank you so much. Here you are.
Security: Welcome to the United States.

Unit 04 | Script

Conversation

Wilma: Is this Fred's car?
Betty: Well, he said it was a big black car.
Wilma: Look inside! What a mess!
Betty: There're a basketball and some old sneakers in the front seat.
Wilma: The back seat is covered with dog food.

Betty: I'm not sure if getting a ride is a good idea.
Fred: Hello, are you ready to go?
Wilma: Uh, sure, shall we get in…?
Fred: Yep… But that's my car over there.
Betty: Oh, thank heavens… Do you know whose car this is?
Fred: I think it belongs to Barney.

Listen Up

2. Easy Listening

Woman: Hello?
Man: Uh… Is the black SUV parked on Maple Street yours?
Woman: Yes, it is. Is there a problem?
Man: Well, yes, there is…
Woman: Oh, is it blocking your car? I'll be right down.
Man: Wait a moment… Your car isn't blocking mine.
Woman: OK, may I ask why you are calling?
Man: Actually, your car windows were open, and it started to rain.
Woman: Oh, really? I will be down as quickly as I can.
Man: Don't hurry. I covered them with some plastic.
Woman: Oh, thank you so much…

3. Hard Rock

DJ: Good evening, one of our listeners needs your help tonight. Thank you for coming.
Woman: Thank you.
DJ: How can our listeners help you?
Woman: I'm looking for my little dog.
DJ: Where did you last see him?
Woman: He was running down the main street Friday afternoon.
DJ: Would you please describe him?
Woman: He's small and brown. His left eye is missing and he's blind in the right eye.
DJ: It sounds like he's had a hard life.
Woman: Oh, he also has a limp when walking. His name is Lucky.
DJ: I hope we get lucky and find Lucky.
Woman: If anyone sees him, please call 012-345-6789. Thank you!

Unit 05 | Script

Conversation

Diana: Excuse me. Is there a flower shop around here?
Kevin: Yes, there's one around the corner.
Diana: I'm new to the area. Could you be a little more specific?
Kevin: Sure, walk straight and turn left at the corner. You'll see a big convenience store. The flower shop is between the convenience store and the bank.
Diana: Oh, thanks. One more question… Is there a jewelry store nearby?
Kevin: I'm not sure, but ask Cathy in the flower shop. She can help.
Diana: Thanks so much.

Listen up

2. Easy Listening

A: Excuse me, can you help me find a movie theater?
B: I'm sorry I don't know where it is. There is a taxi cab stand over there next to the bank, and they can usually help.
A: Oh thanks… Excuse me, can you help me?
C: Sure, what can I do for you?
A: I'm looking for a movie theater.
C: Humph, are you joking?
A: No, I need to find the movie theater. Can you help or not?
C: Just turn around. You're standing right in front of it.
A: Oh… Thanks.

3. Hard Rock

Come on down to Best Buy. We have sales on everything in the store. Save up to 25% on all selected items. For a special giveaway this Friday, the first 100 customers will be entered into a draw to win a 50% off coupon for anything in the store. Take subway line 4 to the Main Street station. We're located 100 meters down the road from exit 7.

Unit 06 | Script

Conversation

Jared: Why are you late today?
Gemma: Honestly, I woke up late.
Jared: What time do you usually get up in the morning?
Gemma: I get up at seven every morning.
Jared: What time do you leave for work?
Gemma: I usually leave at 8:15.
Jared: Do you take the bus or the subway to get here?
Gemma: I take the bus.
Jared: Try taking the subway. It is usually faster than the bus.
Gemma: Okay, I'll try that tomorrow.

Listen Up

2. Easy Listening

Woman: Hi, John! How are you today?
Man: Oh, hello Meredith, I'm great. What's new?
Woman: Well, I just won a radio contest for a concert this weekend.
Man: You did? Congratulations!
Woman: Well, do you want to go with me? I won two tickets.
Man: I'd love to! When does the concert start?
Woman: It starts at 7:30 (half-past seven).
Man: What time should I meet you?
Woman: Let's meet at seven, and then we can get good seats.
Man: Why don't we meet at five instead? Then we can have something to eat or talk over coffee first.
Woman: That sounds great.

3. Hard Rock

Woman: Would you help us and take a survey?
Man: Sure, what's it about?
Woman: We want to know about your daily routines with technology.
Man: Okay. Ask me anything.
Woman: How often do you talk on the phone?
Man: I have four or five phone calls a day.
Woman: Do you prefer phone calls or text messages?
Man: Text messages. I don't have to respond to them right away.
Woman: How often do you check your email?
Man: Most days, I check it twice a day. Sometimes more.
Woman: What do you usually do while checking your email?
Man: I usually listen to the news or watch TV.
Woman: Thank you very much.
Man: You're welcome.

Review Units 04~06

Conversation

Jerry: Cindy, have you seen Mango today?
Cindy: Isn't he around here? He was here at lunch time.
Jerry: Yes, he was here when I came home for lunch. We ate lunch at 12 as always. Now I can't find him anywhere.
Cindy: Oh, look there! Mango's coming. He's a mess. There are some flowers in his fur.
Jerry: He must have gone near the flower shop. We usually go there around 5. And a lady at the flower shop always gives Mango a special treat.
Cindy: I think he must have gone there for the special treat.
Jerry: I think so. But I locked him up after lunch, and I don't know how he got out again.
Cindy: Oh, well. That's a mystery.

Unit 07 | Script

Conversation

Cindy: Kimberly brought her new boyfriend to the party last night.
Annie: Oh, could you tell me about him?
Cindy: Well, actually… He's kind of short and a little plump.
Annie: I don't believe it. I thought Kimberly's ideal man was tall, dark and handsome. Not short and round… Okay, then why are they dating?

Cindy: Maybe it's because he's so funny and very stylish.
Annie: Really? Maybe he has a brother that might like me?
Cindy: Sorry, no luck there. He has three older sisters.

Listen Up

1. Getting Ready

a. She's in good shape. With long blond hair and a blue dress, she looks amazing.
b. He's very tall but thin. He's wearing casual clothes.
c. He's muscular but has almost no neck because he exercises too much.
d. She has dark brown hair, beautiful blue eyes, and full lips.

2. Easy Listening

A: Hello Mary, how was your blind date last night?
B: Actually he was really nice but not my type.
A: Tell me about him, what does he look like?
B: Well, he's about average height and little overweight. He has short curly brown hair and startling green eyes. He's a real gentleman.
A: So, are you going to see him again?
B: Probably not.
A: Why not?
B: I just don't think he's my type.

3. Hard Rock

NEWS FLASH, ladies and gentlemen, please be careful of two runaway prisoners. They broke out of the local jail late last night. The man is in his late thirties, about five feet seven inches tall, and 175 pounds with blond hair and blue eyes. He is a muscular man. The other prisoner is a woman in her mid-twenties. She is five feet two inches tall and about 105 pounds. She has brown hair and green eyes. Both are considered armed and extremely dangerous. If you see either one of the prisoners, please call 1-800-555-1234.

Conversation

Andy: What are you up to?
Brad: I'm learning to play the guitar.
Andy: Why are you learning to play the guitar?
Brad: I'm trying to get Jennifer to go out with me. She said she likes musicians.
Andy: I see. By the way, I thought we were going to meet our friends and have dinner.
Brad: Sorry, I lost track of time. Shall we take a walk or get a taxi to the restaurant?
Andy: It's still early. We can walk.

Listen Up

1. Getting Ready

a. The girl is having fun. She's cooking something delicious.
b. See her look of concentration. She can finish painting soon.
c. That looks like fun. He's playing a great video game.
d. The boy is going to hit the tennis ball very hard.

2. Easy Listening

Man: What are you doing?
Woman: I'm checking our mattress. We need a new mattress.
Man: What's the matter with this one?
Woman: I toss and turn all night. Look at these marks on my arms.
Man: What are they?
Woman: They are bites.
Man: Did the cat bite you?
Woman: No. The bedbugs are living in that mattress and bit me.
Man: Okay. Let's get a new mattress.

3. Hard Rock

Do you have a passion for learning? Do you want to learn something new? Come to the community center and take a look at our list of available classes. We offer many activities that you can join and help you keep your passion for learning. We have music classes, art classes, and craft classes at different times. We also have many different physical activities like dancing, badminton, yoga and many, many more for you to participate in. Come and check it out at our office or on our website at www.communitycenter.com!

Unit 09 | Script

Conversation

Shannon: Rachel, what do you think about this blouse?
Rachel: It's nice, Shannon. But this one's prettier.
Shannon: Wow, look at the price! It's the most expensive blouse here.
Rachel: But I think none of these look better than this one. I want to buy it, but I can't. I don't have enough money.
Shannon: Well, let me buy it for you.
Rachel: You are the most generous person I know. But, I…
Shannon: Your birthday is in a few weeks… It's an early present.
Rachel: Oh, thank you!
Shannon: You're welcome.

Listen Up

1. Getting Ready

a. It's wonderful to go on a hike in the country.
b. This is the scariest thing we've ever done, but I love roller coasters.
c. A couple is sitting quietly on the beach.
d. Skydiving is a thrilling adventure.

2. Easy Listening

A: Mary, what do you think about Matthew?
B: I don't like him much. He's talkative and easygoing… And I heard that he's the pickiest eater.
A: Picky? I heard he is a vegetarian.
B: Well, that does make him a picky eater.
A: Okay. Do you know if he's generous?
B: I heard he's kind of generous. Sarah, why are you asking about Matthew?
A: Oh, because he asked me out on a date this weekend.

3. Hard Rock

It is the trend to buy the biggest item sets. Buying house items in bulk is cheaper per item. That one item might cost you $1.00, and buying 20 of them almost costs you $15.00. You can save money by buying more. But here's the point you are missing. If you buy things in bulk and don't use all of the items, then you're throwing your money away. Do not buy bulk items if you won't use them all. Buying cheaper and bigger will save you money, but only if you're going to use it.

Review Unit 07~09

Conversation

Shannon: Wow, Annie, we're shopping on Rodeo Dr.
Annie: I know some of the stores here are the most expensive stores in the world.
Shannon: What do you want to shop for?
Annie: I don't know. Hey, look at the couple who are walking toward us. Isn't that Brad and Angelina?
Shannon: No way. Brad's taller and more muscular… And Angelina is a lot thinner.
Annie: I guess you're right. But they did look like them… a little…
Shannon: No, they didn't! Are you feeling okay?
Annie: It's just a little hot. Why don't we go get something cool to drink?
Shannon: Sounds good.
Annie: And let's take a walk after that. Maybe we'll see another famous face.

Unit 10 | Script

Conversation

Lilly: Hey, James. What's wrong?
James: My car has a flat tire.
Lilly: What happened? What did you do?
James: I don't know. I went to a shopping mall with John yesterday afternoon.
Lilly: Did your car have a flat tire there?
James: I don't think so. It was fine when I was driving to John's house after shopping.
Lilly: Did you go through any construction zone?
James: Oh, yes… Maybe my car had a flat there.
Lilly: Did you fix your car?
James: No, not yet. I just left it at John's house.

Listen Up

1. Getting Ready

Yesterday, it was windy in the afternoon. I sat on the bench in the park. Suddenly it started to rain, and a strong wind blew my umbrella inside out.

2. Easy Listening

I am Chris. In 2005, when I was 20 years old, I was living in Toronto with my parents. I was studying piano at college. Last year, I taught students at a community college. I worked hard. It was an excellent job. Last month, I was in Vienna on a business trip. I played the piano in three concerts. They were all fantastic.

3. Hard Rock

Man: Hello, would you like to take a survey?
Woman: Sure, what's the survey about?
Man: We want to know the last time you did these activities.
Woman: Sounds interesting… Ok.
Man: When did you last visit a museum?
Woman: That was last year sometime. It was after I saw a museum movie, maybe eight months ago.
Man: When was the last time you got a haircut?
Woman: I got a haircut last week actually.
Man: When was the last time you were in the hospital?
Woman: Last year, I slipped on some ice and broke my leg.
Man: Sorry to hear that. What did you do last night before bed?
Woman: I read a book about self-improvement.
Man: Thank you very much.

Unit 11 | Script

Conversation

Mina: Josh, you are a sportsaholic.
Josh: Why do you think so? I just love playing tennis with you.
Mina: Okay, but what else do you play? Let's see, you play basketball on Mondays and Thursdays.
Josh: Yeah, and soccer on Saturdays.
Mina: Oh, and you go golfing almost every Sunday.
Josh: What can I say? I love sports.
Mina: And that's just summer sports. In winter, you do even more…
Josh: I know I love snowboarding, ice skating, skiing, and so much more. They're great.
Mina: I know you do. It's just too bad you're not good at any of them.
Josh: Ouch, that hurts.

Listen Up

1. Getting Ready

a. This sport can be played as a team or one on one. It requires two rackets, a ball, and a net.

b. This can be played solo or as a group. It's played with one heavy ball and ten pins.

c. This game must be played as a team. It requires nine people. If you get three strikes, and you are out.

d. This game requires two rackets and a shuttlecock. Some people use a net to play it.

2. Easy Listening

A: Bill, do you know when the soccer game starts?
B: It'll be broadcast after the news.
A: Yeah, but the news ended ten minutes ago.
B: Did you try a different channel?
A: Of course, that was the first thing I checked.
B: I don't know, it should be on right now, Friday night at 7 p.m.
A: Let me see. Well, we're early for it.
B: What do you mean?
A: This is next week's schedule.

3. Hard Rock

Man: What are you going to do this weekend?
Woman: I am going to stay at home and practice my music.
Man: What instruments do you play?
Woman: I started playing the piano when I was eight. Now I can play the violin and the trumpet.
Man: That's amazing. I wish I could play music. I was an athlete in school.
Woman: Let me guess. You were a basketball player, right?
Man: No, I couldn't shoot the ball. I was good at golf.

Woman: Is that why you like wearing collared shirts so much?
Man: You got it.

Unit 12 | Script

Conversation

Everyone: 3… 2… 1… Happy New Year!
Jim: Do you have any plans for next year?
Becky: I want to take a lot of pictures. How about you?
Jim: I am going to practice the cello, start a diet, and go to your photo exhibition.
Becky: My pictures aren't that good.
Jim: Of course, they are. You have a great eye for photography.
Becky: If you say so… How about traveling with me this year? We can go anywhere.
Jim: Alright, let's go someplace warm.
Becky: Now you're talking! How about the Caribbean?
Jim: Oh, that's a great idea. I'm already excited for the trip.

Listen Up

2. Easy Listening

Man: Hello, would you like to sign up for one of our exercise and diet support groups for the New Year?
Woman: What kind of exercise groups do you have?
Man: Mountain Biking and Cross Country Biking are our most popular.
Woman: I don't have a bike.
Man: That's OK. The course includes buying a new bike if you need one.
Woman: How often does it meet?
Man: It meets on Saturdays and Sundays.
Woman: I can't. I have church on Sundays. Thanks for offering anyway.
Man: No problems, take this flier in case you change your mind.

3. Hard Rock

Jacob: Greetings, Val!
Val: Oh, hi Jacob. What's that smell?
Jacob: I don't know what you are talking about.
Val: You've been smoking again, haven't you?
Jacob: It was only one cigarette… OK, I just can't quit.
Val: Have you tried seeing your doctor or an e-cigarette?
Jacob: I've done both of those.
Val: Well, maybe the price increase will help you stop. I heard a pack of cigarettes is now $10.
Jacob: Actually, it's $13, and It'll will be $15 in a few months…
Val: Anyways, I can support and help you if I can. Don't give up.
Jacob: Thanks, Val.

Review Units 10~12

Conversation

Becky: Josh, what happened?
Josh: Oh, I broke my arm last weekend.
Becky: How did it happen?
Josh: Well, last Friday, Mina and I went roller skating. And we fell down a lot.
Becky: I thought you can skate very well.
Josh: Not really… To make matters worse, it even started to rain.
Becky: Did you slip in the rain?
Josh: Yes, we did. But that wasn't how it happened. We had a good time.
Becky: Okay, then what happened?
Josh: I was washing the dishes after dinner. I hit my elbow on the sink. That's how I broke my arm.
Becky: Oh… You should be more careful in the future.
Josh: Don't worry. I'm going to be more careful.

Vocabulary

Unit 01

country
nationality
flag

German
British
Korean
Turkish
Kenyan
Chinese
Indian
Canadian
Brazilian
American

Unit 02

doctor
instructor
police officer
actor
designer
taxi driver
photographer
commuter programmer
singer
chef
busboy
barista
babysitter
cashier
librarian

Unit 03

possession
planner
mechanical pencil
DSLR
wallet
bike
glasses
lap top computer
backpack
cell phone
CDs

in
at
on
by
next to
beside
behind
in front of
under

Unit 04

car
couch
jacket
basketball
DVD
sneakers
coffee machine
guitar
hat
refrigerator

hairy

wooden
barking
cute
round
flying
bouncing
leather
rectangular
cooling
wheel
freezing

Unit 05

park
jewelry store
convenience store
dentist
movie theater
mall
student center
bookstore
parking area
cafeteria
hospital
drugstore
bank
bakery
shopping mall

Unit 06

good
beautiful
important
delicious
friendly
comfortable
big

short
small
new
young
ancient
round
muscular
heart
red
dart
white
French
Korean
lunar
wooden
cotton
paper
roasting
sleeping
walking

get up
talk over coffee
have lunch
read a book
send a text message
talk on the phone
check e-mail
take a shower
go jogging
watch TV

work
smoke
make
get up
travel

go to the theater

go out for dinner
go camping
go to a drive-in movie
extreme sports
sporting Event
visit a museum
go to an amusement park

always
usually
often
sometimes
occasionally
rarely
never

wake up
check your email
take a shower
read a book
exercise
go shopping
listen to music
eat lunch
go to sleep
watch TV

Unit 07

young
middle-aged
old
elderly
child / children
teenager
adolescent
adult
short
medium height
tall
petite

muscular
well-built
fit
skinny
thin
slim
slender
underweight
plump
stocky
overweight
blond
curly
straight
brown
dark
fair
pale
tanned
handsome
pretty
beautiful
good looking
healthy-looking
ugly
moustache
beard

Unit 08

meet friends
play computer games
play the guitar
cook dinner
check blogs
work out
take a walk
have a drink with
clean the room
study

Unit 09

tight
loose
quiet
talkative
picky
easygoing
generous
mean

cheap
cheaper
cheapest
picky
pickier
pickiest
expensive
more expensive
most expensive
good
better
best
bad
worse
worst
many
more
most
little
less
least
far
farther / further
farthest / furthest

Unit 10

drive a car
get a haircut
take pictures
take a bus
see a doctor
hang out with friends
see a movie
do homework
take pictures
get a haircut
go shopping
cook dinner
study English

Unit 11

play the trumpet
play baseball
play the violin
play tennis
play soccer
ski
play golf
play ice hockey
play basketball
fence

Unit 12

travel
go on a date
go on a diet
learn the cello
graduate from college
get married
buy a new bike

Note